WEEKEND**escape**

BRUSSELS

Brussels:
the secret city

Like the River Senne that flows through it, Brussels is a secret, hidden city full of unexpected sights and attractions. Although it may not reveal its charms at first, it has much to offer, amuse and interest its visitors. Among the capitals of Europe, it remains unfairly underrated, yet Brussels is a city that'll happily open its heart to you if you're prepared to give it the chance.

Home to the Surrealists and the Brueghels, the city of Brussels has a feast of delights on offer. Grand-Place and its surrounding area is known as the 'belly of Brussels' – an art nouveau jewel, a tower of Babel and the capital of Europe, whose inhabitants both love and loathe it. You may have to turn a blind eye to the disfiguring building sites and try not to notice its chaotic lack of urban planning, which has laid waste whole neighborhoods, but since it gained independence as a capital of a divided country, Brussels has constantly looked to the future. People are

moving back to the city after a worrying period of desertion and can be found decorating their house-fronts in brilliant colors and filling their window boxes with beautiful flowers. The city center has been

revived by a handful of restaurateurs, fashionable designers and bar-owners, with new and ever more attractive establishments opening every week. Spending a lot of time indoors throughout the year, the people of Brussels have become geniuses at interior design. The city's art nouveau architecture, for which Brussels was famed in the prosperous days of the early 20th century, is once again drawing approval. Victor Horta's residence and the Van Eetvelde hotel have been restored. A superb Andalusian-style resisdence, which long stood derelict, has been transformed into a cultural center and the wrought ironwork on a group of quaint old shops has finally been repainted in honor of the arrival of the Musée des Instruments de Musique. The city's inhabitants are friendly and hospitable. With barely one million residents in total, and more green space per inhabitant than any other European city, Brussels is not overcrowded. Its dozens of tree-filled parks lend a country air to the capital which many other cities might envy.

russels extends far beyond
he area contained within
he pentagon formed by its
4th-century ramparts. The
9 'communes', or districts,
utside the walls have merged
vith those inside to such an
xtent that the uninitiated
ever notice which part they're
n, whether it's Brussels-Ville,
xelles, Saint-Gilles or Forest.
n fact, only the born-and-bred
nhabitants of the Marolles
istrict can truly claim to be
rom Brussels. These rebellious
haracters, whose colorful
pinions are expressed entirely
n the local *brusseleir* dialect,
re always a tourist attraction
t the flea markets. In fact,
russels has an interesting
atchwork of neighborhoods.
rom working-class Marolles
o aristocratic Sablon, from
he tourist center of Grand-
lace to trendy Saint-Géry,
ou can quickly move from

ne atmosphere to the next.
t's also a cosmopolitan,
nultilingual city, where half
he population is foreign,
nany from other parts of
Europe. In the same street, for
xample, you'll find an
talian delicatessen, a Greek
estaurant, a Spanish *bodega*
nd a traditional Belgian
riterie (hamburger stand).
This diversity creates a
gourmet's paradise, as the
restaurants compete to
produce the most imaginative
combination of cuisines and
flavors from around the world.
The city is also an Aladdin's
cave for connoisseurs of
antiques and ethnic artifacts.
People come from far and wide
to scour the bric-a-brac and
antique shops for bargains.
Once inside these places it's
hard to leave without making
a purchase. Fashion is also
important in Brussels.
Designers such as Olivier
Strelli, Dries Van Noten,
Dirk Bikkembergs, as well as
Ann Demeulemeester, whose
talents have been noticed
abroad for several years now,
live and work in the city.
Christophe Copperns conjures
up the wildest hats imaginable
and the new second-hand
dealers excel in the art
of turning old into new.

Whatever the weather, a night
out in the fashionable bars
and clubs will warm you up,
but the cafés are where you'll
find that image you've had in
mind all weekend: the
irrepressible beer-drinker from
a Brueghel banquet or one of
Magritte's chess players. From
chocolate to Surrealist art,
from fashion to secondhand
comics, Brussels, once visited,
is a city to which you'll want
to return, again and again.

Practicalities

Decide upon your weekend dates and your means of transportation, make the arrangements… and off you go! Once there, you'll still have to choose between scores of museums, restaurants and stores. Whether your penchant is for chocolate, comics, architecture or beer, what Cocteau called 'the most beautiful theater in the world' is yours.

The climate

Considering it rains at least 200 days a year, don't forget to take your macintosh or umbrella. The other 165 days may be dull, grey, cool… or very hot. Winters are rather mild and damp, spring sometimes pleasant, and in summertime heatwaves sometimes roll in. If you're looking for bargains, you should know that sales start from July 1 and January 1. The theater season takes place from September to May, but festivals in Flanders and Wallonia also attract music lovers in summer. You can obtain information from the tourist information center on Grand-Place (main square – Bruxelles-Tourisme ☎ 00 322 513 89 40); Brussels offers a wealth of events, festivals and shows all year round.

Before you leave

Tourist offices UK
29 Princes Street, London
W1R 7RG
☎ 020 988 7799
(Brussels–Ardennes)
225 Marsh Wall, London
E14 9FW
☎ 0800 9545 245
Tourist offices US
Suite 1501, 780, Third Avenue,
New York NY 10017
☎ 212 758 8130

The tourist information center give out a brochure of genera information about Brussels, a detailed map of the city center, a subway map, an explanatory leaflet about the hotels and a guidebook to the restaurants, all free of charge. As well as a yearly calendar of main events, you can find out more about the shows, exhibitions and other important happenings. Get as much documentation as you can from the overseas tourist offices, because you'll have to pay for the same documents once in Brussels. Do not hesitate, either, to browse on the web sites of the Brussels tourist information office:

www.brusselsinternational.be
www.Belgique-tourisme.net
www.agenda.be
These sites are regularly updated, and will enable you find out information and to learn about the latest cultural events.

Last but not least, if you are going with your children, be sure to to check out www.paluche.org where many activities for children are listed.

How to get there

By sea/car

Hoverspeed
www.hoverspeed.com
Dover to Ostend: regular departures throughout the day.

Transeuropa Ferries
www.transeuropaferries.com
Ramsgate to Ostend: four departures a day.
To drive from Ostend to Brussels, take the A10/E40 (approximately 70 minutes).

PUBLIC HOLIDAYS

January 1: New Year's Day
Easter Monday
May 1: Labor Day
Ascension Thursday
Whit Monday
July 11: celebration of the Flemish Community
July 21: national holiday
August 15: Assumption
September 27: celebration of the French community
November 1: All Saints' Day
November 11: Remembrance day (Armistice WW1)
December 25: Christmas

P&O North Sea Ferries
www.poferries.com
Hull to Zeebrugge: one departure a day; crossing time 14 hours. To drive from Zeebrugge to Brussels, take the N31 and E40 . The journey takes approximately 1 hour 15 minutes.

By plane
From the UK

The following are the main airlines flying direct to Brussels from London, although there are many smaller ones with direct flights from regional airports.

British Airways
☎ 0870 850 9850
www.britishairways.com

British Midlands
☎ 0870 6070 555
www.flybmi.com

SN Brussels
☎ 0870 735 23 45
www.flysn.be

Easyjet
☎ 0870 6 000 000
www.easyjet.com

Ryan Air
☎ 0871 246 0000
www.ryanair.com

From the US

The following airlines fly direct to Brussels from the US:

SN Brussels
☎ 516 622 2248
www.flysn.be

American Airlines
☎ 0800 221 1212
www.americanairlines.com

United Airlines
☎ 0800 242 4444
www.united.com

Delta Airlines
☎ 0900 525 0280
www.delta.com

Continental Airlines
☎ 800) 525-0280
www.continental.com

By train

The Eurostar train links London and Brussels in under three hours several times a day. Trains arrive at the Gare du Midi in Brussels. Information and reservations:
www.eurostar.com

The Thalys train links Paris and Brussels in about an hour and a half (www.thalys.com). When reserving in advance, you will benefit from fares as much as 50 percent lower, but with limited choice of schedules. Try to reserve your seat two to three weeks beforehand, as fares double for peak days and times.

From the airport to the city center

Zaventem airport is located 14km (8.5m) northeast of Brussels. To go to the city center, you have three possibilities: train, bus or taxicab.

Train

The fastest and cheapest means is the train which takes you to the central station in 25 mins. Departure every 20 mins from 5.18am to 11.48pm (from 5.30am to 12.20am during the week) from the station in the basement of the terminal. Tickets are available at the ticket offices open from 6.45am to 9.45pm (€2.60 for a one-way ticket).

Bus

On leaving the airport you'll notice a bus stop. The n°12

WEEKEND PACKAGES

Travel agents, tour operators, airlines and ferry and rail companies all offer 2–3 day weekend packages including transportation and different category hotels. In most cases, you need to include a Saturday night in the package. If you are coming from the UK, the main advantage of this kind of package is the stay in a luxury hotel at a discount price (Royal Windsor, Métropole, Amigo, Plaza) and the convenience of having the agent arrange all your travel reservations and tickets. However, you should be aware that, apart from luxury hotels, the selection of hotels is quite limited and the 2- and 3-star ones tend to be 'tourist factories' which welcome groups all the year round.

bus of the STIB reaches the Schuman traffic circle in 30 minutes (connection with the subway). Departure every 20 minutes from Monday to Friday from 5.45am to 11pm, every 30 minutes on Saturdays, and on Sundays every hour. The bus stop is in front of the arrivals hall. The ticket can be bought from the driver and costs €3.

Taxicab
The cab will take you to the entrance of your hotel for about €30. Allow from 30 minutes to an hour for the journey.

Car rental
You'll get better value if you reserve before you leave. In Belgium, at the airport (arrival hall), at the station, and in the city center, you will find car rental agencies displaying very different tariffs. It is up to you to compare the prices and the advantages on offer. Don't forget to ask for the weekend tariff and be careful if you park in the city center: the tow

SOME HINTS ABOUT PRICES

From €13 to €30 for a meal, drink included; from €2 to €5 for entrance to a museum; €1.30 for a tram ticket; from €1 to €1.50 for a coffee or a beer; from €3.80 to €5 for a cocktail or a glass of spirits; from €5 to €13 to get into a nightclub; from €5 to €13 for a seat in the theater or a concert; from €7.50 to €11.20 a cab ride in Brussels. As for shopping, you may well be tempted by the delicious chocolates (pralines), a wide range of strong beers with matching glasses, as well as cartoon books, CDs and antiques, all of them far less expensive than in many other parts of Europe.

trucks are quick to tow away badly-parked cars!

Note that **Europcar** offers the best weekend tariffs. Information at Brussels, Gare du Midi:
☎ (00 32) 25 22 95 73

Entry procedures
EU citizens should carry a valid ID card or passport. Non-EU citizens will require a valid passport, although US citizens do not require a visa to enter Belgium. No vaccinations are necessary.

Belgian Embassies

US
3330 Garfield Street
N.W. Washington,
DC 20008
☎: 202 333 6900
www.diplobel.us

UK
103-104 Eaton Square
SW1W 9AB London
☎: 020 7470 300
www.diplobel.org/uk

Canada
360 Albert Street, Suite 820
Ottawa, ONT, K1R 7X7
☎: 613 236 7267
www.diplomatie.be/ottawa

possible cancellation of your trip and medical repatriation. Find out more from your credit card company or ask your bank. EU citizens can also reclaim medical expenses once back in the UK; make sure you take an EHIC with you (available from post offices). Non-EU citizens should make sure they have adequate cover. The cost is low but it offers real benefits in case of problems.

The Belgian euro

All the prices are of course displayed in euros. Since January 1 2002, the Belgians have given up their francs and adopted the European currency. At the conclusion of a contest organized by the European Commission, the design of Luc Luycx, a graphic artist for the Royal Mint of Belgium, was selected for the motif of the European side of the coins. As for the national side, it bears the image of His Majesty Albert II, the King of Belgium, showing his left-side profile. The royal monogram (a crowned capital A) is also represented between the 12 stars symbolizing Europe. This creation is the work of Jan Alfons Keustermans, the

Australia
19, Arkana Street, Yarralumla, ACT 2600, Canberra
☎: 2 6273 2501
www.diplomatie.be/canberra

South Africa
158, Jan Smuts Building Walters Avenue, 9, 3d floor West Core, Rosebank
☎: 11 912 9600
www.diplomatie.be/johannesburg/

Customs

For travelers returning to other EU countries, there are few restrictions on alcohol or tobacco products. The only stipulation is that the goods must be for personal use and guidelines are provided, for example 10 liters of spirits, 90 liters of wine and 800 cigarettes. Duty-free limits for travelers leaving the EU are as follows:

Alcohol over 22%: 1L *or* alcohol under 22%: 2L *and* still table wine: 2L.
Cigarettes: 200 *or* cigars: 50 *or* tobacco 250gm.
Perfume: 60ml.
Toilet water: 250ml.

Insurance and Health

If you pay for your ticket by credit card, you automatically benefit from some insurance regarding your luggage, the

FESTIVALS AND FAIRS

February: Fair of Belgian Antiquarians
March: International Festival of Fantasy Film
Late April-early May: Royal Greenhouses at Laeken open to visitors
May-June: Queen Elizabeth International Music Competition
June-July: Brussels European Film Festival
July: Ommegang (procession and feast in honor of Charles V of Spain)
August 15 (on years of even date): Carpet of Flowers
Early December: Christmas Market

director of the Municipal Academy of Fine Arts in Turnhout.

Budget

Life in Brussels is probably a little less expensive than it is say in Paris, except for restaurants. When you have paid for the hotel and transportation (from €90 to €280), you will have to allow a budget of about €140 to €220 (for 2 days) to spend on restaurants, evenings out, museums, concerts and cafés. It depends of course on your choice of venues and the number of times you stop off in bars! What is indisputable is that to have a coffee or a beer on the terrace of a café is very reasonable in Brussels as, unlike France for example, there is no difference in price whether you are standing at the bar or sitting on the terrace. Last but not least, the bars do not add a surcharge at night, which is a real godsend for midnight revellers.

HINTS FOR SAVING MONEY

• During the weekend, thousands of European Union civil servants leave the city to go back home and the big hotels are left empty. Don't reserve in advance, but as soon as you arrive go to the **Office de Promotion du Tourisme**, rue du Marché-aux-Herbes. You will be offered luxury hotel rooms at considerably reduced prices.

• **Arsene 50** offers concert seats and shows at half price on the day, provided you collect the tickets in Brussels before 5.30pm Tue.-Sat.

Ticket offices: Théâtre du Vaudeville, galerie de la reine and at Flagey, place Sainte Croix.
See also www.arsena50.be.

Useful websites

www.brusselsdiscovery.com
The official website of the Brussels Tourist Office.
www.belgianstyle.com
Includes a guide to the many types of Belgian beer and where to drink them.
www.noctis.com
Information on nightlife in Brussels.
www.trabel.com
Detailed information about travelling within Belgium.

Local time

Brussels summer time is 2 hours ahead of GMT; winter time is GMT + 1 hour.

Voltage

The current is 220 volts in Belgium and the plugs are round two-pin continental European. You will require an adaptor and possibly a transformer to use North American or British electrical equipment.

Chocolate heaven

Whether you're a reckless chocoholic or a gourmet who'll eat only the darkest bitter chocolate, make sure you try Belgian pralines. Inside the white, milk or dark chocolate shells the fillings of nuts, creams, liqueurs or simply more chocolate will melt in your mouth with unforgettable flavors. You'll have to decide for yourself which of the chocolate makers is the best – just don't count the calories!

Cocoa or *cacahuatl?*

On their return from America the conquistadores brought back plants that were unknown in Europe, such as the potato, the tomato and cocoa. As they had no names for these plants, they also imported a few Aztec words to the Spanish court. 'Cocoa' is a phonetic transcription of the pre-Columbian Nahuatl word *cacahuatl*, which comes from the Maya word *cacau*, whereas the Aztecs called their chocolate drink *xocatlatl*.

A drinkable currency

Children who love to eat chocolate coins may be very surprised to know that the Maya and Aztecs paid for goods in cocoa beans. They also had the secret of a delicious drink, which was very nourishing according to the conquistador Hernan Cortez, who tasted it for the first time in 1519 at the court of the emperor Montezuma. The Aztecs ground up grilled cocoa beans

and added either vanilla, cinnamon, nutmeg and honey or green maize, or fermented agave juice and pepper to make a luxury drink reserved exclusively for the nobility.

The taste of sin

The Spanish improved the Aztec recipe by adding sugar, and soon none of them could do without their chocolate, even monks and nuns. All the monasteries and convents in New Spain had a special place for making chocolate. Questions were asked, however, as to whether these servants of God should be drinking chocolate, as it was said to heat the blood and encourage the desires of the flesh. It's interesting to note, therefore, that it was the nuns of Puebla who invented the particular recipe of turkey with chocolate, known as *mole poblano*.

Sweets for the élite

It was Anne of Austria, daughter of Philip III of Spain, who brought cocoa beans home in her luggage in 1615, and introduced chocolate to the people of France. From there it made its way to England and in 1657 the first chocolate house opened in London. Chocolate as a beverage became the rage of the 17th-century London elite. From London to Madrid, Paris to Brussels, it remained a luxury until the 19th century.

Chocolate for all

In 1815, Kaspar van Houten discovered a process for separating part of the natural fat of the cocoa bean to produce cocoa butter and a more digestible product that could be reduced to powder.

The chocolate industry was born, aided by the fact that by this time cultivation of the cocoa plant had spread to Asia and Africa. Belgium's conquest of the Congo in 1885, under Leopold II, provided the Belgian chocolate industry with new opportunities. In 1910 there were 73 chocolate manufacturers, whose production, strictly controlled by the state, established a reputation for fine quality.

Pralines and ballotins

The praline, invented by confectioner Jean Neuhaus in 1921, is a small confection containing a nut or other sweet filling, covered in a thin chocolate coating. To stop them from being damaged in the traditional paper cone, Neuhaus created a new type of packaging, a small cardboard box called a *ballotin*. Chocolate bars of 30 and 45gm (10½ and 15¾ oz) were invented by the Belgian Kwatta Company.

The chocolate-maker's secrets

The chocolate used for coating is richer in fats but not as sweet as the finished product, and, processed into the form of liquid or drops, is used for making cakes and pralines. Two elements are vitally important if the final product is to have the right aroma and flavor: these are the origin of the beans (they can be either Criollo, Trinitario or Fonastero), which are then combined in proportions kept secret by the manufacturer; and the way that they are ground.

PIERRE MARCOLINI

His passion for chocolate led him all around the world to select the best raw cocoa with a view to developing a product entirely by cottage industry. In the luxurious *malline*, the assortment of ginger, pistachio, green tea and violet pralines is an enthralling sight for the eyes before the tastebuds are captivated. An imaginative excellence that will delight true chocolate lovers!

1, rue des Minimes (Grand-Sablon)
☎ **02 514 12 06**
Sun.-Tue. 10am-7pm, Fri. and Sat. 9am-8pm.

Home of comics

Cradle of the modern comic, homeland of Tintin, Spirou, Gaston Lagaffe, Alex the Cat and others, Belgium celebrated a hundred years of the cartoon strip in 1997. The country produces 40 million comic books a year, of which 11 million are sold in Belgium. So why this fascination with cartoons, and how come this small country has the highest density of comic writers and illustrators per square mile in the world?

Pictures that talk

In a country where two languages and two cultures co-exist (not to mention the continual influx of invaders of various kinds, which continued right up to the 19th century), visual language has had a deep impact on the population, who strive to communicate against all odds. In the 1950s Belgium was the country with the highest number of cinemas outside the USA. This attraction to the language of images and to the visual arts in general is no doubt one reason why Belgium has become the center of the comic strip.

Hergé the pioneer

On January 10, 1929, the first adventure of a reporter called Tintin appeared in *Le Petit Vingtième*, the Thursday supplement of a Brussels' daily paper. It became so successful that in 1930 Hergé published the complete adventures of *Tintin in the Land of the Soviets* in the form of an album. The idea that a comic could be published as a book, with a proper hardback cover, and be kept on a shelf to be read and re-read, became one of the innovations of Belgian comic production.

The cult of the hero

Tintin is an open and somewhat asexual character who could be placed in a wide range of settings. Though he was a colonialist in 1930, by 1975 he was siding with the guerillas.

Characters in the newer comics often traded the role of the tough-guy hero for that of a more vulnerable, human figure with whom the reader could more easily identify.

Schools of Brussels and Marcinelle

By the 1950s Belgian comic production had polarized around two centers: Editions du Lombard in Brussels, with *Le Journal de Tintin* (*Tintin's Diary*) and the Dupuis company in Marcinelle, which launched the oldest comic in Belgium, the weekly *Spirou*, in 1938. Some have defined these two as schools, particularly the school of 'clear lines' in Brussels. But in fact this simply reflects the impact of Hergé's powerful personality. He imposed a certain style on his collaborators, whereas the *Spirou* cartoonists around Jijé (Franquin, Peyo, Morris, Roba) were freer to establish their own different personal styles.

The clear line

The phrase 'clear line' appeared in the 1970s and is used to define a style invented by Hergé. In practice, this type of drawing was a technical necessity due to the poor production qualities of the *Petit Vingtième* newspaper. After the Second World War, this weekly supplement was replaced by *Le Journal de Tintin*, which was published in color on better paper. This publication centered around Hergé, with future big names of the comic strip, including Jacobs, Martin, De Moor and Tibet.

Second wind

When Tintin and Spirou's readers grew up they had nothing to read. However, 1959 saw the launch of the French magazine *Pilote,* headed by Goscinny. This at first targeted teenagers, but gradually evolved as its audience got older. This more mature audience for comics continued to grow and in 1978, in the Belgian town of Tournai, Casterman brought out the first issue of the monthly comic *À Suivre*. This featured work by both Belgian artists and the world's greatest comic-strip authors, becoming a showcase for the diversity of contemporary comics.

The comic charts

'For young people from 7 to 77'. Today this slogan, coined by the *Tintin* magazine, is more relevant than ever, since comics have grown up with their readers. There are now a wide range of titles with a huge readership. But though adult comics make up a major sector of the specialist magazine market, the titles with the widest circulation are still *Lucky Luke*, *Bob et Bobette* and *Asterix*.

The comic strip in the city

In view of the dilapidated state of the houses in the city center, the cartoonists mobilized to decorate whole walls. Ric Hochet, Victor Sackville, Lucky Luke, Boule and Bill can all be discovered as you stroll along. Don't miss the Schuiten passageway in Rue du Marché.

LE CENTRE BELGE DE LA BANDE DESSINÉE

By taking over the former Waucquez department store, an art-nouveau gem designed by Horta in 1905, the museum saved the building, which was scheduled to be demolished to make way for a car park. It was furiously defended by a group of comic fans and eventually became home to a museum devoted to comics. The displays are very educational, retracing the history of the comic strip with original plates: the Belgian pioneers from 1929 to 1960 and major trends from the 1960s to the present day, in Belgium and abroad. The exhibition of original plates is regularly changed for reasons of conservation.

20, rue des Sables – Bus 38 from De Berlaimont or metro Gare Centrale, Rogier or Botanique. Access via stairs from Boulevard Pacheco. ☎ 02 219 19 80 Tue.-Sun. 10am-6pm, closed 1 Jan. and 25 Dec.

André Breton

Brussels
surrealism

After a few hours in the European capital, you'll realize that it has a slightly puzzling atmosphere. In this improbable city, created from a patchwork of 19 districts full of contrast and contradiction, you never know when you'll come upon something out of the ordinary. It's not hard to understand why Brussels inspired Surrealist painters like Magritte and Delvaux.

From Paris to Brussels

1924, the year André Breton published the *Surrealist Manifesto* in Paris, also saw the birth of Surrealism in Brussels among a group of poets and artists. It grew out of their common feeling of 'rebellion against the world that is allotted to us and against the given, which is always humanly unacceptable'. It was primarily an ethical movement. When Magritte saw a reproduction of the *Song of Love* by the painter Giorgio de Chirico it was a revelation to him.

The visions of Magritte

Magritte came from the lower middle-class and lived all his life with his wife Georgette, together with a Pomeranian dog. Uniquely, he would paint in his living-room in a suit and bow tie. He was also a writer and poet, who never supplied any clues to understanding his art. His only message was that his pictures should be seen as lessons and they should give the viewers a sense of mystery, making them feel as if fantasy and reality were continually combining, an emotion he experienced throughout his childhood and youth. By continually playing with the processes of synthesizing and deconstructing our ideas about objects, he was able to place our own vision of the world in doubt.

Naked women and trains

Paul Delvaux painted in a style very different from Magritte. Much maligned by Magritte, Delvaux's work is the fruit of his own natural outpourings, rather than the result of a desire to uncover a different kind of reality. His recurring landscapes, filled with temples, wandering women, skeletons, trains and unanswered appeals, form an obsessional interior landscape. His images of anxiety (1938-1940) were followed by the strange paintings of a dreamer always filled with wonder.

A Surrealist café

La Fleur en Papier Doré was one of Magritte's favorite cafés. A framed photograph shows the owner, Geert Van Bruaene, with Magritte and his friends from the Society of Mystery, including the poets Elt Mesens, Louis Scutenaire, Paul Colinet and Camille Goemans. 'Long live Lautréamont' (a pre-Surrealist writer) is written on the wall in capital letters, along with aphorisms and pictures by the café owner, who was a fervent admirer and supporter of the Surrealists. The many kitsch objects were part of his dream concept, consisting of things whose uselessness made them poetic. 55, Rue des Alexiens, ☎ 02 511 16 59).

Surrealist hallucinations

Although Delvaux rarely visited the art-nouveau café

Ultieme Hallucinatie (316, Rue Royale, ☎ 02 217 06 14), its interior could come straight out of one of his paintings. The wooden carriage seats in the winter garden, designed by Henry Van De Velde for the Belgian railway company SNCB, are arranged around tables and a caravan awning with a sky-light. A ghostly female nude, which haunted Delvaux's nights, stands in the garden,

Saint-Michel Cathedral

turned to stone. Sadly, the waterfalls which once graced the gardens of the Mont des Arts, where the Surrealists spent time engrossed in cryptic conversations, have been replaced by a cold acropolis.

'Façadism'

'Brusselisation' was followed by a new era, the age of 'façadism'. In this period the

old buildings were still being destroyed, but a small part of their façades would be preserved. These would then be shored up and integrated into a modern construction, just like something painted by Magritte.

Deciphering the city

The wide boulevards change their name depending on the side of the road you're on and the road leading to Mons is identical to the one leading to Bergen, for this is in fact the same city, Mons being the French name, Bergen the Flemish one – very confusing! Since 1989 Brussels has been the capital of Flemish-speaking Flanders, although 86 percent of the city's inhabitants speak French. The monumental law courts have a dome 100m/330ft high and a 3,600m²/4,000sq. yard waiting hall. But it's the Gothic St Michel Cathedral which houses the Flemish community and its proximity to a sort of futuristic remake, bristling with steel tubes, that takes the prize for surrealism.

SURREAL SUMS FOR THE "BERLAYMONSTER"

How surreal! In 1990 it was discovered that the Berlaymont built in 1963 to house the European Commission was tainted by asbestos. The Belgian state then calculated that a renovation, costing 160 million francs, would be the least expensive solution. After 14 years of work that cost ten times as much as the initial budget, the Commission at last found itself re-housed in a building covered with glass. A small detail: it could now house only 2,000 of the 19,000 civil servants that work for the Commission!

Art nouveau

By the early 20th century the population of Brussels had doubled and was stifling inside its medieval walls. King Leopold II decided to bring some air into his capital by building suburbs and creating two wide, shady avenues, Avenue de Tervuren and Avenue de Louise. These became the favorite haunts of the bourgeoisie, who commissioned the building of grand eclectic residences – a true celebration of renewal.

Economic boom

The reign of Leopold II was a period of great prosperity. Belgian industry was expanding and the Congo, which the king had bought in 1885, was a source of enormous riches, including precious woods and ivory. The new middle classes were liberal, enlightened and progressive. They turned their backs on the old values, asserting their independence and the originality of their new ideas by encouraging a wide range of experimentation in architecture, mainly featuring new materials such as iron and glass.

Personalized houses

Art nouveau was seen as a liberating revolution against the tedious similarity of the old 19th-century façades which, even when they were intended to be ostentatious, turned out to be depressingly monotonous. Paul Hankar was one of the first to reject this mediocrity by designing houses that were all different, with wide doors and windows topped with colorful arches. Another major figure, Victor Horta, abandoned the plan of three interconnecting rooms, which still characterizes many houses in Brussels, bringing light into the heart of the home.

A marriage of technical skill and imagination

In the 19th century, Japan was reopened to the outside world and the influence of its sober, pared-down art spread far and wide. This, combined with the new industrial technologies and the importation of marble and precious woods from the Congo, stimulated the architects to experiment with designs for flexible, modern housing adapted to the needs of its inhabitants. Free of the old constraints they turned to plants and Gothic designs for inspiration.

A house-cum-manifesto

With its narrow façade galvanized by an all-glass bow window, the overt use of iron with its rivets clearly visible, and its yellow and blue stonework, the Hotel Tassel, built by Victor Horta in 1893, remains a key building in the history of architecture. In particular, the way that the rooms are laid out around a superb spiral staircase and the decoration – including the famous 'whiplash' – reveal the genius of the man who was to become a leader of the art nouveau movement.

Luxury and sensuality

With the support of his industrialist friends, Horta

was given an entirely free rein to design art nouveau's most striking buildings, of which the Hotel Solvay is the finest and most luxurious. Horta considered every single detail: he chose all the materials himself, from mahogany from the Congo to padauk from Burma, and designed everything down to the smallest elements of the decor, including radiators and door handles. It goes without saying

that the wallpaper, carpets and furniture are all unique and were specially designed to suit each room.

Towards modernism

Henry Van de Velde, who started out as a painter, was utterly opposed to the extravagant fantasy and proliferation of decoration to

which Horta's followers were too often prone. Rigor, minimalism and purity of line were his watchwords, making him a forerunner of the design movement. After a stay in Germany, where he headed the school that would become the famous Bauhaus, in 1926 he opened La Cambre Institute of Decorative Arts, still open today and very highly regarded.

Palais Stoclet

Built between 1905 and 1911 by Viennese architect Josef Hoffmann, this building marks the end of the period of exuberance and fantasy. Its refined façade, pronounced straight lines, covered with marble and discreet bronze decoration, reflects the movement towards art deco. Unfortunately the interior, decorated by Klimt, is not open to the public (271-281, Av. de Tervuren).

SERRURIER-BOVY, ART AND INDUSTRY

Art nouveau was undoubtedly an elitist art. Gustave Serrurier, a cabinet maker from Liège, wanted to mass-produce his furniture. Although he managed to set up a business employing around a hundred workers, he didn't make a lot of money, as potential customers demanded unique items. But collectors appreciate the simple geometric shapes of the Serrurier-Bovy furniture fashioned from wood and metal.

The Brussels spirit

The experience of sharing their city between two peoples, the Walloons and the Flemish, and coping with the presence of foreign invaders has endowed the citizens of Brussels with a mistrust of principles, the capacity to ignore authority and a wonderful sense of humor, known as *zwanze*, which enables them to laugh at just about anything.

The first *zwanzer*

At the height of the Spanish occupation, it was Brueghel the Elder, an inhabitant of Marolles, who first practised the art of *zwanze* in his painting. At first sight *The Massacre of the Innocents* is just another biblical scene, but it's set in a village on the outskirts of Brussels and Herod's soldiers are wearing the despised uniform of the Duke of Alba. Besides criticizing Spanish violence, Brueghel also portrayed everyday life with sympathy and humor – look as long as you like, you'll never find the husband among the excited revellers in his famous painting *The Wedding Feast*.

Puppets and Mannekenpis

A puppet that tells *flauwskes* (silly jokes) every evening at the Théâtre de Toone, and the statue of a little boy relieving himself on a street corner, are the true heroes of Brussels. They are far more famous than Dukes d'Egmont and de Hornes who led an uprising against Philip II of Spain and were beheaded on Grand-Place, although Mannekenpis *did* sprinkle water on a bomb which threatened to blow up the city hall! King Louis XV of France was not without wit and gave the statue an embroidered coat to ask forgiveness for the bad behavior of his soldiers, who had stolen the statue in 1747.

A city without perspectives

Search all you like, you won't find a single perspective view in Brussels. The Royal Palace is approached from the side; the great thoroughfare of the Rue de la Loi turns its back on the arch of the Cinquantenaire; what you see at the end of the famous Avenue de Tervueren is not the famous Central African Museum but a private house. Saint-Michel Cathedral is wedged between tall, modern apartment blocks and the view of Grand-Place is hidden by a series of hotels built in an ersatz 'old' style. Brussels has deliberately decided not to show off its monuments to good effect. It's up to you to try and find the best angle for a photograph!

Out and about in Marolles

Round, jolly faces, toothless or ironic grins, beer drinkers leaning on the bar or sleeping at an alehouse table – here you'll find all the rogues and beggars captured by Brueghel. Not long ago you could still witness some truly burlesque scenes, such as closing time at Le Bossu, when the owner would untie the rope stretched across the room and on which

her drunken, drowsy clients were draped like washing. If you'd like to get a flavor of the local *brusseleir* dialect, drop into Le Coq (32, rue de Montserrat, ☎ 513 33 56), the last authentic café in Marolles, and listen to the very vocal elderly locals. It's the best way to get an idea of their very particular kind of humor, and even if you can't understand a word they're saying, you can still

soak up the atmosphere along with your beer.

Brusseleir dialect

The real Brussels' *zinneke* ('bastard') is the only Belgian for whom the quarrel between Flemish and French simply does not exist. Living in a city hated by the Flemish, who don't feel at home here, and rejected by the French-speaking Walloons for supporting the

Jacobins in the French Revolution, the *zinneke* speaks the colorful Brusseleir dialect, a mixture of Flemish and French, with words taken from the languages of the various occupiers, such as *moukère* (*mujer*) meaning 'woman'.

The *estaminet*

With its polished wood and gleaming pumps, this is the quintessential meeting place. It's here that Belgians come to imbibe a good proportion of the 264 pints/120 liters of beer they each drink on average in a year. But remember: The way the beer is served is a very serious matter. Each type has a corresponding glass of the best possible size and shape, a correct temperature and a way of pouring that doesn't shake up the yeast deposit. And if the owner wants a boring customer to leave, he simply places a metal figurine, known as a *zageman*, on his table.

TINTIN AMONG THE BELGIANS

There's always an element of Hergé's humor that just can't be explained to Tintin's non-Belgian readers. Did you know that in reality the Picaros and the Arumbayas spoke the same language? That King Ottokar IV's motto is 'Eih Bennek, Eih Blavek' ('I'm here, I'm staying' in the Brussels dialect) and that Colonel Spons is Colonel Sponge? French speakers could always try reading Tintin with the *Dictionnaire du dialecte bruxellois* (Louis Quiévreux).

Lambic and *gueuze*,
the local brew

Of the 400 or so varieties of Belgian beer, there is one whose flavor cannot be that different from the brew drunk by the ancient Egyptians and Sumerians 5,000 years ago. *Gueuze* beer is a drink halfway between wine and beer, produced through spontaneous fermentation. A long process of aging in the cask gives it a depth and subtlety that completely disproves the myth that beer is a drink lacking in refinement. *Gueuze* is the pride of Brussels. It is the last beer still to be brewed using a process of spontaneous fermentation following Pasteur's discovery of the secret of yeast in the 19th century.

Stage one: brewing

The grains of wheat (35 percent) and malted barley (65 percent) are first crushed before being poured into a vat of water heated to a temperature of 72°C. After two hours the saccharification process converting the starch into sugar is complete and the wort (a sweet deposit of malt and wheat left at the bottom of the vat) is pumped into large boiling vats

containing rotating blades. At this point hops (at least three years old to avoid any excessive bitterness) are added in greater quantities than in other beers. This facilitates the preservation of the beer and gives it its flavor. The beer is boiled for three hours and loses about a quarter of its total volume through evaporation, but this raises its sugar content, and therefore its alcohol content.

Fermentation from natural culture

The liquid is then pumped into large, shallow basins located in the well-ventilated roof space of the brewery, where it cools overnight, passing from a temperature of 95° to 20°C (203° to 68°F). This is the magic moment when the culture forms spontaneously, brought about by naturally occurring ferments, including *Brettanomyces bruxellensis,* which is present in the air of the Senne valley. It is these ferments that give lambic its unique taste. Now all that remains is to move the precious liquid into oak or chestnut pipes (650 liters/178 gallons) or barrels (250 liters/69 gallons).

The *Lambic* emerges

After a few days a spontaneous process of fermentation begins, in which the wort is transformed into alcohol and CO_2. For the first four weeks this is so rapid that the barrels cannot be closed due to the risk that they might explode. Fermentation gradually slows down and becomes more complex over a three-year period, producing a flat beer with an acidic taste and subtle flavors that develop in your mouth. This drink is known as *lambic*. It can be drunk in its pure form at the brewery or in a very few cafés in Brussels (La Bécasse) which sell it in sufficient quantities, as it starts to lose its quality once the barrel is opened. You can also buy a variety known as *faro*, consisting of lambic with added cane sugar.

Gueuze, the champagne of beers

To obtain *gueuze* beer, the master brewer selects five or six lambics which are one, two and three years old. The younger ones provide the natural sugars necessary for further fermentation, while the older ones give the beer its refined smell and taste. After fermenting further in the bottle over several months, the *gueuze* becomes sparkling and acidic, with a flavor not unlike cider. The taste varies from year to year and according to the blend. The most unusual versions are those where fruit is added to the beer. Morello cherries picked in late summer are soaked in a two-year-old lambic for three months before it is bottled. The slightly acidic beer that results is called Kriek. This is a real delight, very refreshing and with an almond aftertaste. The heady, sparkling and strongly flavored raspberry beer is the pink champagne of beers.

A LIVING MUSEUM: BRASSERIE CANTILLON

Of the dozens of breweries that have plied their trade in Brussels since the sixteenth century, only two small producers, one of which is the Cantillon family, have avoided being taken over by the big national groups. Making real *gueuze* beer takes a lot of time and money. It can be brewed only in the cold season, from October to April, and only about 18 brassins or 1000 hectoliters (250 gallons) a year are made. But the finished product is totally different from Bellevue's industrial *gueuze*. If you're in Brussels during the cold season make sure you go on a tour of the Cantillon brewery. You may be lucky enough to be present at a morning's brewing and in any case you'll get an opportunity to taste the product.

56, rue Gheude – Bus 47– Liverpool stop, or underground tram – Lemmonier stop. ☎ 02 521 49 28 Mon.-Wed. 9am-5pm, Sat. 10am-5pm. Entry charge.

Brussels
in bloom

With its 4,000ha (10,000 acres) of parks and woodland, amounting to a quarter of its entire area, Brussels is second only to Washington, USA, in the list of the world's greenest cities, leaving aside the many private houses that have gardens. As you wander through its green spaces you'll realize that people in Brussels tend not to be great fans of brick and concrete, instead they are people with a true passion for nature.

Brussels in flower

The flower season opens in April in the old botanic gardens, where you can gaze at the magnificent beds planted with 2,500 irises of 40 different varieties. In May, the Royal Greenhouses of Laeken open to the public. Under the glass and iron domes designed by A. Balat in 1887, the tropical forest of giant palm trees, coconut trees and tree ferns is adorned with a riot of seasonal colors, azaleas, hydrangeas and fuchsias. Grand-Place is entirely covered in a wonderful carpet of begonias for the holiday weekend of 15 August.

From park to park

The Parc Royal in the very center of the city, with its geometrical design dotted with mythological statues, the unexpected Egmont park, hidden behind the Hilton hotel, and the great park of Cinquantenaire are all havens of peace, much appreciated by the citizens of Brussels. Yet there are other parks that are just as attractive, some of which even the locals don't really know about. Tervueren, with its large lakes and an arboretum, is the most popular destination for a Sunday walk. Tournay-Solvay Park in Boitsfort, with its romantic, neo-Renaissance ruined château, has a fine rose garden, while vast Duden Park (23ha/57 acres) in Forest is a wild wood. Lastly, Josaphat park in Schaerbeek is planted with rare species such as the Virginia tulip tree, and is decorated with a number of ornamental lakes and rockeries.

An art deco garden in Uccle

Like most of the inhabitants of Brussels, the Van Buurens, who were collectors and patrons of the arts, couldn't imagine having a house without a garden. Their own garden stretches for more than a hectare (2½ acres) behind their art-deco house and was designed as an extension of their home. Like the building's bay windows and the furniture inside it, the hundred-year-old maples, wild lemon trees and mineral elements in this picturesque garden, which was designed by J. Buyssens, reflect a

Japanese influence. You can also lose yourself wandering through the maze of 300 yew trees that leads to the seven leafy chambers illustrating the *Song of Songs*.

Semi-wild places

Fifteen minutes from the city center, between Molenbeek and Jette, a series of inter-connecting, swampy open spaces have been miraculously preserved within this urban area. You can cycle or walk through the 126 ha/310 acres, ranging from vegetable plots to meadows, woods and marshland full of frogs, herons and kingfishers, where you're also quite likely to spot a fox or two.

The forest of Soignes

This vast forest, with its magnificent, towering beeches two hundred years old, stretches for 4,380 ha/10,800 acres to the south of the city. Its grassy hollows, ruined abbeys such as Rouge-Cloître and many lakes have all provided inspiration for painters and poets. La Cambre wood on the edge of the forest, created in 1862 to plans by the German designer E. Keilig, is a particularly fine

example of landscaping. La Cambre abbey with its 14th-century church, 16th-century cloister and tiered gardens is one of the most attractive places in the city.

Secret garden

Thierry Boutemy
2a, rue de la Pépinière
(Metro: Porte de Namur)
☎ 02 649 39 49
Tue.-Sat. 11am-5pm
In his small baroque boutique, where water burbles in a stone basin, Thierry Boutemy, from Honfleur in France, creates works of ephemeral beauty. He lovingly produces wonderful compositions using wild flowers, which he buys every morning from the small market gardens around Brussels. Primary colors and subtle, woody scents mingle in these little bouquets, which will fill your home with their lasting perfume.

DON'T MISS

Les serres de Laeken (Royal Greenhouses of Laeken)
Avenue du Parc-Royal – Tram 23, 52 ; Bus 53 (Gros Tilleul) ☎ 02 551 20 20 ou ☎ 02 513 89 40
Open to the public two weeks a year (generally end April-early May).
Musée David et Alice van Buuren
41, avenue L. Errera – Bus 60 ; Tram 23, 90 (Churchill roundabout)
Museum and garden: every day except Tue. 2-5.30pm.
☎ 02 343 48 51 – www.museumvanbuuren.com
Entry charge.
An exceptional residence of the 1930s.

King of
the Belgians

In 1830 Belgium became independent, but had neither a constitution nor a head of state. After several months of debate, the European powers organized the election of a National Congress, which chose a prince of the Saxe-Cobourg-Gotha family as king. Leopold I swore his coronation oath on 21 July 1831. So what is this royal family, whose members seldom appear in the press?

Chronicle of a royal death

The sudden death of King Baudouin in 1993 plunged the whole of Belgium into mourning. For two days nearly 50,000 people filed past his body as it lay in state. The Belgians were caught between sorrow and confusion, which was a surprisingly excessive reaction when you think that there had been absolutely no visible trace of royal influence on Belgian politics throughout the king's 42-year reign. But still the Belgian people showed their affection.

Leopold II

Orphan Belgium

Deprived of any executive power when his father Leopold III abdicated following the Royal Question, Baudouin, who was crowned on July 17, 1951, was condemned to become a shadowy figure, whose only power was over the appointment of the Prime Minister. The slow fragmentation of his kingdom, which became a federal state in 1992, gave him a dual role of mediation and conciliation. 'The cement of Belgium', 'Father of the Nation' cried the press the day after his death, as though the very survival of Belgium depended on him.

Albert and Paola

As King Baudouin died leaving no children, everyone expected his nephew Philippe to be crowned. He had been preparing to take over from his aging uncle for years. But in the end it was his father, Baudouin's younger brother, Albert, who became the 6th king of the Belgians. Since then, Philippe and Mathilde have been installed in the palace at Laeken, while Albert and Paola reign from the Belvédère. The storm has passed and the palace has returned to its routine. Although Paola has no specific role, she assists the king in the exercise of his duties by attending state occasions and ceremonies, involving herself in charitable work and, with her strong interest in art history, safeguarding the preservation of Belgium's artistic heritage.

Château life

No changing of the guard, no fashionable receptions, no grand balls, no processions or waving from carriages, and above all no scandals. The Belgian monarchs keep themselves very much to themselves, with none of the trappings of royalty. If Louise and Stéphanie, the daughters of Leopold II are to be believed, château life was anything but fun, even if their father was thought to have had a few amorous adventures. It was only after the death of his wife Marie-Henriette that he introduced his mistress, a young Frenchwoman called Blanche Delacroix, known as 'Baronne de Vaughan', who

gave him two sons, Lucien and Philippe.

A hereditary passion for cars

Leopold II was the first of the royal family to be an interested visitor to the Paris Motor Show. He owned several powerful Mercedes, which he tended to drive rather fast. Since his day the press have continually referred to the royal passion for expensive cars. Apparently, Baudouin used to drive his car up and down the avenues in the grounds at Laeken, never daring to pass through the gates. His brother Albert has always been more interested in motorbikes.

Mathildomania

Philippe maintains that it was on his own initiative that he met Mathilde d'Udekem d'Acoz, who he married in 1999. Moreover, this young lady with a devastating smile fitted the five criteria defined by the Belgian court as credentials for the spouse of the heir apparent: to be blonde and smaller than Philippe, to be fluent in both national languages, to have blue blood and to prove that she was a Catholic. Not content with having already given him two children, Elisabeth and Gabriel, Mathilde has managed to make her husband and the

royal family look younger. There is still a fine future for monarchy.

A VERY BELGIAN COMPROMISE

King Baudouin, a devout Catholic and husband of the equally devout Fabiola, faced a terrible crisis of conscience when the Prime Minister asked him to sign a new law decriminalizing abortion. He felt unable to continue on the throne and, on April 4, 1990, he abdicated ... for 36 hours; just long enough for ministers to set their own signatures to the offending text.

Underground
art

Having buried its museum of modern art, Brussels now also puts contemporary works on show in the metro. Perhaps there is no room on the surface for modern artistic expression, or perhaps contemporary art is easier to understand a few feet underground.

A museum in the basement

Following an argument between the preservers of the architectural heritage and those who advocated building a modern art museum near Place Royale, it was decided to build the museum underground. A 65,000m³/ 85,000 cu. yd hole contains seven floors of galleries, arranged in a semicircle around a well of light. This very beautiful building by the Belgian architect Roger Bastin was opened in 1984.

Modern art on the walls

When does modern art begin and end? Although the museum's collections don't contain many works by foreign artists, they do give a good representation of Belgian painting and sculpture from the end of the 19th century to 1940. The 19th-century artists include James Ensor, Navez, Stevens, De Braekeleer and Van Rysselberghe. The fauvist colors of Rik Wauters, Spilliaert's maritime reveries, the mystical images of Laethem-Saint-Martin and the Flemish expressionists occupy a large part of the early 20th-century galleries. Major works by Magritte and a few by Delvaux reflect aspects of surrealism in Belgium. Works by Victor Servranckx, a forerunner of abstract art, who began painting non-figurative works in 1917, are also shown.

The Cobra group

The short-lived Cobra movement, named after the

begins, the kind you can sometimes see in museums, but more often are in private galleries. In the absence of any real policy for buying works by living artists, the city of Brussels has taken the praiseworthy step of asking some well-established and highly respected Belgian artists to provide decorations for the metro, which opened in 1976.

some cities of its artist members (**Co**penhagen, **Br**ussels, **A**msterdam), was the last manifestation of northern expressionism and gave rise to one of the liveliest currents in post-war art. The Cobra artists advocated spontaneous gestures and drew on different influences including untrained and primitive' art, cinema and writing. Dotremont, who co-founded the movement in 1948, advocated non-specialization and experimented with 'word-paintings' with Alechinsky. (Metro Anneessens.)

different approaches to art: Delahaut experimented with color in a minimalist style while Bury explored the possibilities of optical and kinetic art, rejecting any expression of feeling. (Metro Montgoméry or Metro Bourse.)

Art on the metro

Hyperrealism, constructivism, action painting, neo-figuratives, neo-fauvists... there are as many terms as there are artists. The best way to find out about them is to see their work by taking a trip on

Abstract art

Delahaut and Pol Bury, co-authors of the *Manifesto of Spatialism* in 1954, had

After 1958

This can be seen as the point where contemporary art

the metro. From station to station for €1.40, the price of a metro ticket, you can explore the work of the painters and sculptors who have used the environment (speed, the underground world) to make works that have a synergy with the space around them.

ART TICKET

Start your trip at the Montgomery station, where Folon's *Magic City* offers a menacing vision of the future, while Pol Mara shows stereotyped images from our own time in six panels. The ceramics on the wall are by Jo Delahaut. On line 1A, at Thieffry station, you can see Félix Roulin's human bodies trying to free themselves from a flow of molten bronze. Continue on line 1 to Botanique to admire *The Last Migration*, a monumental flight of the imagination by sculptor Jean-Pierre Ghysels, and the twelve multicolored travelers by Pierre Caille. Then take the pre-metro to Bourse, where Delvaux's images of old trams contrast with the slow movements of Pol Bury's steel cylinders. Continue for one more station, and you can complete your tour with an exploration of *Les Sept Écritures*, the beautiful 'logograms' by Dotremont and Alechinsky at Anneessens station.

Behind the scenes
in Europe's capital

As a market town founded over a thousand years ago on the route from Bavai to Cologne, now the capital of a young state riven by quarrels over language, what future would there have been for Brussels without the signing of the Treaty of Rome in 1957? Brussels gave itself to Europe because it couldn't carry on by itself, isolated between Wallonia and Flanders. But there was another side to the coin: Europe brought with it inflated housing costs, depopulation, congested roads and deep scars to the city's already mistreated urban fabric.

Strasbourg or Brussels?

Much is at stake in the rivalry between the two cities, as the economic effects of the presence of the European institutions and the activities associated with them bring in billions of euros each year to Brussels. This is one major reason why Strasbourg is not about to give up its Euro MPs. However, Brussels has recently built all the necessary infrastructure. Apart from the old Berlaymont in its new

glass cladding costing 1.6 billion euros, 1995 saw the opening of the Council of Europe, an enormous granite bunker covering

200,000m²/50 acres, followed in 1997 by the enormous CIC conference center, a 600,000m²/60 acre building designed to house the new

semicircular Parliament…
but only for supplementary
sessions!

Unpopular
civil servants

No matter how many times the
people of Brussels are told that
the presence of the European
Commission is a blessing, the
fact remains that they find the
lifestyles of the European civil
servants extremely irritating.
Their very large salaries,
supplemented by a great
many privileges such as
accommodation allowances,

relocation expenses, tax
immunity and exclusive access
to duty-free shops, are all
sources of resentment for the
ordinary citizens, who pay
very heavy taxes out of their
modest salaries. This has
created a divide between the
population and the Eurocrats,
who show a certain disdain for
their hosts, but are nevertheless
greatly appreciated by the city's
restaurant-owners, hoteliers
and shopkeepers.

Speed is the priority

Since 1835, when Brussels
opened the first railway in
Europe, Belgium's politicians
have wanted to make the city
into the continent's center. In
1900 entire neighborhoods

were flattened to create the
major junction between the
Gare du Nord and the Gare du
Midi, which are 2km (1 mile)
apart. The work was started
under Leopold II and the
junction was opened under
Baudouin 50 years later in
1952. The stations are
currently undergoing their
third facelift to accommodate
the high-speed TGV trains. The
city's ringroads and high speed
routes should make Brussels
easier to get to, but when you
get to the end of the motorway
there are no road signs to tell
the lost traveler how to get to
the city center.

An urban planner's
dream

Among architects the term
'Brusselization' is synonymous
with the destruction of the
urban fabric, an implicit
criticism of the attitude of the
Belgian politicians who
destroy the old to make way
for the new. Sadly they are
spoilt for choice when it comes
to awarding the annual
'golden bulldozer' award to
the most effective destroyer of
the country's heritage. No
surprise then that the term
archietek has become a bit of
an insult.

Little Manhattan

In the late 1960s Vanden
Boynants, head of the
department of public works,
and the property developer
Charly de Pauw dreamed of
transforming Brussels into a
little Manhattan. On the
pretext that the city needed a
new European dimension,
53ha/130 acres behind the
Gare du Nord were flattened to
build the World Trade Centre.
Twenty-five years later this
lucrative operation consists
of four towers randomly
spaced among the cranes on a
vast empty space 1km (½ mile)
from Grand-Place. There
aren't even any offices for
the Eurocrats.

BRUSSELS COMMITS HARA-KIRI

The arrival of the European institutions dealt the death-
blow to a city that had already been gutted. The Léopold
district, much favored by the bourgeoisie around 1850,
was flattened by the bulldozers. Its beautiful residences
gave way to huge, hideous postmodern towers, thrown
up in a hurry, with no overall plan and linked, after the
event, by walkways. A real treasure-hunt for newly
arrived Eurocrats trying to find their meeting-places in
Breydel, Charlemagne, Juste Lipse or Caprice des
Dieux. Yet the Résidence Palace, an art deco jewel
dating from 1926, owes its survival to these same
Eurocrats, who are the only ones now allowed to
dive into its magnificent swimming pool.

Delvaux,
a love of leather

There are two companies that still indulge in the luxury of producing leather items entirely by hand – Hermès in Paris and Delvaux in Brussels. Buying a Delvaux bag is an expensive undertaking, but it's also a gift that you can keep for the rest of your life without worrying that it'll ever go out of fashion. In fact the *Brillant* model, designed for Expo '58, is still the famous brand's best-selling bag.

From luggage to handbags

The company, founded by Charles Delvaux in 1829, targeted its products at wealthy customers who needed solid leather baggage and high-quality travel items for their long transatlantic crossings, chaotic journeys in Pullman cars and trips to spas. In 1933 the business was bought by Franz Schwennicke, who steered it in the direction of its current production of luxury leather goods to accompany designer clothing.

A collection is born

Six months! That's how long it takes for a new design to come into being, from the first sketch to the creation of the prototype. When the designer has finished drawing the piece a first version is made up and any technical adjustments and refinements made. It takes

three months to make one of these models using 'salpa', a mixture of cardboard and leather onto which the tooling is drawn.

A highly specialized craft

Whether they're paring down the leather in preparation for sewing or folding, threading the edges using Indian ink and paraffin or sewing together pieces that have already been glued, the exceptional quality of finish is determined by the skill of the craftspeople who work on it. It takes two years to train machinists, after which they are able to tool the leather without visible joins and can guide the needle on the machine to create the famous saddle stitch.

Calf or ostrich?

High-quality skin is obviously of prime importance. Calf skin and the skins of farmed ostriches and crocodiles are the most highly prized, with a clear preference for smooth or grainy calf. Ostrich skin with its characteristic texture (each bead marks the place where a feather has been plucked) acquires a lovely sheen as it ages, unlike crocodile skin, which dulls. This characteristic,

added to the fact that the process of treating the skin on the flesh side takes a very long time, explains why ostrich skin is so expensive. An ostrich skin bag is three or four times as much as a calf-skin one.

A justified price

When you realize that a piped bag is first designed entirely inside-out and then turned and lined with lambskin, that it takes fifteen return trips from the gluing table to the machinist to put a bag

together, and that it takes between six and thirteen hours' work to make each bag, the price of this luxury item is put into its proper perspective.

Extremely exclusive

Apart from very particular shades such as *rosso* (burgundy), *ravello* (rich brown), daffodil yellow or airforce blue (blue-grey), Delvaux also invented *toile de cuir* or 'leather cloth'. This is a weave of fine strips of leather on a polyamide chain. Infinite variations are possible by altering the thickness and color of the weave.

By appointment to the Court

Since being awarded the quality mark of Court supplier in 1883, Delvaux has had a specially favored relationship with the Gotha family. Paola carried her first crocodile bag, a gift from Delvaux, at the time of her engagement to Prince Albert in 1959. Its role on this occasion gave the bag the name *Le grand bonheur* ('great happiness') and it is still one of the classic bags today. When Paola became queen she remained a faithful Delvaux client.

How to look after your bag

Don't leave leather out in the sun, wipe away any splashes of water immediately, treat greasy stains using talcum powder after you have removed any excess grease with paper tissue and regularly moisturize your leather bag with an appropriate cream. For more serious accidents Delvaux (see p. 101) has now opened a restoration service which can perform small miracles!

ADDRESS:

27, bd de Waterloo
(Metro: Porte de Namur)
or 31, galerie de la Reine
(Metro: Gare Centrale)
☎ 02 513 05 02
Mon.-Sat. 10am-6.30pm.

Practicalities

Getting around

Most tourists spend three hours on average visiting Brussels, as they assume the city is limited to Grand-Place and mussel-and-fries restaurants, but it's important to realize that to get a good idea of the city, which spreads much further than the Pentagone, you need to spend at least two days here. To find your way around, you should be aware that Brussels is divided into six territories. The Pentagon corresponds to the outline of Brussels-City

MORE INFORMATION

You will find route maps for all the walks in this chapter at the head of each tour, and references to sights which also appear in the Don't Miss section.

(that is of the ramparts or the 'small ring'). The 19 districts refer to local entities which surround Brussels City. There is not need to take your car to move around the city center: parking places are rare and the police are particularly quick to impound cars. After parking in the free zones (next to the canal, for instance), you can easily visit the city center on foot, because distances between places are not huge.
If however you intend to follow the 'art nouveau' or the 'Cinquantenaire' routes, make sure, as soon as you arrive, you buy a STIB card in a subway station. It will enable you to take any means of public transportation.
If you drive to Brussels, you'll be able to use your car in the evening and on Sundays, and especially to venture into outlying districts where it is

easier to park. Yet it is advisable to have a navigator and a detailed map of the city, roadsigns being quite fanciful or even useless at times.

By subway, tram and bus

Transport runs from 5am to midnight. The center is well served by a subway (*métro*) network (2 lines) and trams running through tunnels (they are called *pre-métro*). To go to areas outside the Pentagone, you'll often have to choose between the tram (rather slow) and the bus. You can get a detailed map in any station. The tickets (€1.40 each) are sold in the subway and by bus and tram drivers. If you intend to move around often, it is better value to buy a day card (€3.80) valid for two people traveling together on Saturdays, Sundays and public holidays, or even a 3/5 card costing €9 (unlimited access to the network for 3 individual days spread over a period of 5 days) or a 5/10 card costing €12 (valid for 5 days over a period of 10 days). There are also 5- and 10-trip travel cards (€6.50 and €9.80). These magnetic cards must be stamped every time you get onto a bus, tram or subway train and are valid for an hour. You can take any type of connection (STIB, DE LIJN, SNCB). They are sold in the subway (counters and automatic ticket-dispensers), in the STIB ticket-offices (Rogier, Porte de Namur, Midi station, Bourse) and at newsstands.

By bicycle
For those who are not put off by inclines, Brussels, built on several hills, offers the opportunity of getting fit. Although the network of cycle tracks does not cover the whole city, you should be aware that a cyclist has right of way and signposts show the one-way streets that can be used in the opposite direction by cyclists.

By taxicab
Very useful to get to the hotel from the station or the airport, taxicabs are quite expensive (€2.35 minimum charge and €1.1 per km (0.6 mile) in Brussels-Centre and the 19 districts; the fare is twice as much outside Brussels). On the other hand, there is no extra charge for luggage and only the minimum charge increases at night, rising to €4.21 from10pm to 6am. Expect to pay about €30 to get to the airport and from €8 to €13.50 for a trip within

Brussels. At the airport, it is better to choose an **Autolux** (☎ 02 411 41 42), as you will get a 20 percent discount provided you take the same company on the way back. In the city, it's better to phone for a cab because taxicab stands are few and far between.

Taxis verts
☎ 02 349 49 49
Taxis bleus
☎ 02 268 00 00
Taxi Hendriks
☎ 02 752 98 00 (equipped to carry disabled people; book 2-3 days ahead).

Good parking
Have enough coins for the ticket machines (€0.10 an hour, from 9am to 6pm/6.30pm). Parking is free on Sundays and from 1.30pm to 2.30pm in Brussels-Centre and in some districts as well. Be careful, underground car parks (€2.10 an hour, €13.80 for 24 hours) close at night from1am/2am to 6.30am/7am. On Sundays, they are open from 12am to 1am or from 5pm to 10pm.

Fourrière Radar :
257, av. de la Couronne, Ixelles
☎ 02 513 38 47
28, rue Reigersvliet, Etterbeeek
☎ 02 649 95 26

How to phone

To phone outside Belgium, dial 00 plus 44 for the UK or 1 for North America and then the area code without the zero, and the number. In Brussels itself, you have to dial the seven digit number, always preceded by the prefix 02. A reduced rate (50 percent) for national calls applies from 7pm to 8am and on Saturdays, Sundays and public holidays as well. If you phone from your hotel room, you will have to pay a rather heavy supplement.

THE ATOMIUM

This molecule of iron crystal composed of nine spheres and magnified 165 billion times was built for the World Fair in 1958. In 2006, after a substantial face-lift, notably by replacing aluminum with stainless steel for the outside layer of the spheres, the Atomium will serve as a setting for exhibitions and will once more display the sparkle of its innumerable little lights, emphasizing its architecture at night.

Boulevard du Centenaire
How to get there: take the Ring West, exit 8 and follow the signs Heysel-Wemmel, Brupark or Expo.
☎ 02 475 47 77
www.atomium.be
1 Sep.-1 Apr. 10am-5.30pm, 2 Apr.-31 Aug. 9am-7pm, closed until January 2006 for renovation.
Entrance: adult €6, child €3.

Telephone booths

Telephone booths are relatively rare and not of a standard design. It is up to you to spot them! However, they are useful as they will cost less than cell phones or hotel phones, particularly for international calls. The boooths work with Belgacom phonecards of €5 or €10. National calls cost €0.30 a minute from 8am to 7pm during the week. For international calls, it is better to use a prepaid card (XLcall, Eurocity) of €5 or €10. All these cards are sold at newsstands and all-night stores.

Cell phones

There are three cell-phone operators in Belgium: Proximus, Mobistar and Base. It is up to you to check with your operator which one offers the most attractive tariffs. If you have to make many calls in Belgium, you should consider buying a local SIM card. The set prices are €15, €25 and €50 (Proximus, Mobistar) and €7, €14 and €28 (Base).

Writing and mailing

Stamps are sold in the post offices(Mon. 9am-6.30pm, Tue.-Fri 9am-5pm). The main post office, located in the Centre Monnaie (bd Anspach ☎ 02 226 39 00) is open from 8am to 11pm during the week and from 9.30am to 3pm on Saturdays. The international tariffs for a 50g letter are €0.55 normal mail and €0.60

priority mail. Letter boxes are red.

Banks

Banks open from 9am to 4pm or 6pm from Mondays to Fridays and some of them from 9am to 12am on Saturdays. You can withdraw money from the automatic cash dispensers with an international credit card (Visa, Eurocard, or MasterCard). Remember to get enough cash before the weekend, as cash dispensers often run out of cash as early as Saturday. Don't worry, though, as most shops accept payment by credit card. If you have an American Express card, go to the office at Gare du Midi station (☎ 02 556 36 00, open every day 6.30am-10pm) with a cheque in your name.

Payment by cheques

If you wish to pay by cheque, whether personal or traveler's checks, inquire before you leave. The fees can be high. It is therefore much better to choose to pay by cash or

credit card. But once again commission may be charged by your bank.

Tourist offices

Bruxelles International

Hôtel de Ville de Bruxelles, Grand-Place-1000
☎ 02 513 89 40
www.brusselsinternational.be
Open every day 9am-6pm (in winter, Sunday 10am-2pm), closed Sundays from January 1 until Easter and on December 25.
You will find information about hotels, restaurants and cultural events in the capital city. Employees are also able to book hotel rooms for you. A very complete guidebook about Brussels is on sale (€2.50) with a map, a restaurant guide, maps of themed routes and some interesting books about art and the history of Brussels. You will also find the Brussels Card (€30 for 3 days) with which you will be entitled to free access to 30 Brussels museums. It includes a transportation pass for all the Brussels network as well as a color guidebook of the city.

OPT Wallonie-Bruxelles
(Office de promotion du tourisme)
63, rue du Marché-aux-Herbes-1000
☎ 02 504 03 90
❶ 02 504 02 70
Mon.-Fri. 9am-6pm (7pm in July and August), Sat. 9am-1pm and 2-6pm (7pm in July and August), Sun. 9am-1pm, from Nov. to Mar. and 9am-1pm/2pm-6pm from Apr. to Oct. (7pm in July and August).

See and talk Brussels

Six associations gathered under the name 'Voir et dire Bruxelles' can help you discover the city from unusual angles. If your French is good enough, you can join in discussions and French-speaking tours; otherwise some events are organized for English-speakers.

Arau : 55, bd Adolphe-Max,
☎ 02 219 33 45, bookings Mon.-Fri. 9am-5pm.
www.arau.org
From April to November, Arau offers you the chance to discover Brussels by coach (on Saturday) or on foot (on Sunday), with the themes of architecture, town planning, social and economic policy.

Arcadia.be :
120, rue Hôtel des Monnaies,
☎ 02 537 67 77
Booking Mon.-Fri. 2pm-6pm
www.asbl-arkadia.be
Art historians will share their passion for Brussels heritage every weekend, from Feb. to Sep. walking tours with different themes: art deco, art nouveau, modernism, Leopold II's achievements or the Laeken Cemetery.

Bus Bavard :
☎ 02 673 18 35
www.busbavard.be
Every day 8am-6pm.
During the weekends from Apr. to Dec., a thematic tour takes place by coach or on foot, focusing on the diversity of the city and its inhabitants.

La Fonderie :
☎ 02 410 99 50
Mon.-Fri. 9am-5pm.
Specializes in industrial heritage, such as a tour around the old slaughter houses in Anderlecht, Brussels harbor, or a chocolate factory. The trips are made by boat, coach or on foot, on Tues., Thurs., Fri., Sat., and Sun., from mid-Mar. to late Oct.

Itinéraires : ☎ 02 534 30 00
Mon.-Fri. 9am-5pm.
www.itineraires.be
Tours from1.30pm to 2pm on Sat. from Apr. to Dec.
Brussels seen through its celebrities, real or imaginary, through its gastronomy and its music.

Pro Velo :
15, rue de Londres,
(Metro: Trône)
☎ 02 502 73 55
www.provelo.org
Every weekend from Apr. to Oct.; by arrangement the rest of the year.
From Apr. to Sept., by day or at night (Sat. 9pm) 12–25km (7.5–15.5 mile) bicycle rides across the capital city and its surroundings according to chosen themes (beer, strip cartoons, green spaces, etc.)

Musée du Transport urbain :
364B, av. de Tervueren-1150
☎ 02 515 31 08
www.mtub.be
From Apr. to Oct. on the 1st, 3rd, 4th and 5th Sunday in the month at 10am, there is a three and a half hour tour aboard a 1935 tram.

Opening times

Most museums open their doors from 9-10am to 5-6pm. The closing day is generally Monday. Beware, some museums close at lunch time and others are only open in the afternoon. Students (on presentation of their cards), children from 6 to 18 and senior citizens (over 60 years old) can benefit from reduced prices. For information:
www.brusselsmuseums.be

USEFUL CONTACTS

Police emergency:
☎ 101.

Emergency: ☎ 100.

Accident: ☎ 105.

SOS Doctor:
☎ 02 513 02 02.

Doctors and pharmacists on duty:
☎ 02 479 18 18.

Dentists on duty:
☎ 02 426 10 26.

Police central station:
30, rue du Marché-au-Charbon
☎ 02 279 79 79.

SOS vehicle breakdown service:
☎ 070 34 47 77.

Lost Property:
Zaventem airport
☎ 02 753 68 20.
Trains (Gare du Nord)
☎ 02 224 61 12.
Tram, bus, metro
☎ 02 515 23 94.

What to see in Brussels
and sights not to miss

To make your discovery of the city easier, we suggest 11 strolls through Brussels, each of them illustrated by a map. If you have only a little time to spend, here are ten sights that are not to be missed on any account. They are all mentioned in this guidebook and you will find more details about them at the end of the *What to see* chapter.

Around Grand-Place

A famous site: admire the Gothic façade of the Town Hall before proceeding to musée de la Ville de Bruxelles. Then treat yourself to some window shopping at the stores of Galeries royales Saint-Hubert.

See walk no. 1, pp. 38-41 and Don't Miss p. 66.

Musée des Instruments de musique

A museum worth visitng for its architecture as well as for its collections. A musical break which will fascinate virtuosos and beginners alike.

See walk no. 5, p. 49 and Don't Miss p. 67.

Musées royaux des Beaux-Arts

Art lovers cannot pass these by. The Royal museums of Ancient and Modern Art contain real treasures. You will be able to admire the famous Flemish primitives and less well-known but equally talented artists.

See walk no. 5, p. 49 and Don't Miss p. 68.

Around Place Royale

A tour to find out a little more about the successive rulers of Belgium. After walking through the former palace of the dukes of Burgundy, and visiting the archeological excavations of the Aula Magna, you will be an expert on this topic.

See walk no. 5, pp. 48-49 and Don't Miss p. 69.

Parc du Cinquantenaire

Golden Jubilee Park is where, among other buildings, you will find the Royal Art and History museums as well as Autoworld.

See walk no. 10, p. 62 and Don't Miss p. 70.

Musées royaux d'Art et d'Histoire

The sophisticated architecture of the Royal Art and History museums habors collections that will please the most diverse tastes. Archaelogy, decorative arts or non-European civilizations are displayed here.

See walk no. 10, p. 62 and Don't Miss p. 71.

Maison Cauchie

Built in 1905, maison Cauchie offers a wonderful mix of pictorial scenery and interior architecture. After this visit, *sgraffiti* will no longer hold any secrets for you.

See walk no. 10, p. 63 and Don't Miss p. 72.

Centre belge de la Bande Dessinée

A magnificent art-nouveau building which relates the history of the strip cartoon. The star is of course the inescapable Tintin!

See Culture and Lifestyle p. 13 and Don't Miss p. 73.

Le musée royal de l'Afrique centrale

Thanks to the rich collections of this Museum of Central Africa, you will feel you know everything about the history, the fauna and flora, and the customs of the region.

See Don't Miss p. 74.

Musée David et Alice van Buuren

The art deco style of the van Buurens' house was the work of artists from different parts of Europe. The result of this melting pot is superb. Explore the gardens and the maze as well.

See Culture and Lifestyle p. 23 and Don't Miss p. 75.

1

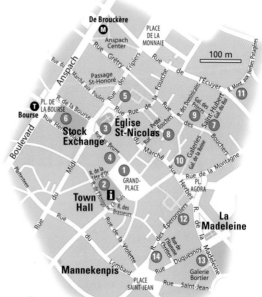

De Brouckère
Anspach
Center
PLACE
DE LA
MONNAIE
Rue du Marché aux Poulets
Rue Grétry
Rue des Fripiers
Rue de l'Écuyer
R. Mont. aux Herbes Potagères
Passage
St-Honoré
Rue du Persil
Rue de la Fourche
Rue des Dominicains
Gal. des Princes
Saint-Hubert
Gal. de la Reine
11
PL. DE
LA BOURSE
Bourse
Rue de la Bourse
R. de la Bourse
Rue Henri Maus
5
Rue au Beurre
Église
St-Nicolas
Rue Petite au Beurre
Rue des Bouchers
9
Galeries
Gal. de la Reine
7
Bouchers
Stock
Exchange
6
3
8
Boulevard Anspach
Rue du Midi
R. de la Tête d'Or
Rue Plattesteen
Marché aux Herbes
10
Rue de la Montagne
4
2
1
GRAND-
PLACE
PL.
AGORA
Town
Hall
R. des
Brasseurs
Rue du Lombard
Rue de la Violette
R. des Éperonniers
R. de la Madeleine
12
La
Madeleine
Mannekenpis
PLACE
SAINT-JEAN
Rue de l'Étuve
Rue du Chêne
14
Rue Duquesnoy
13
Galerie
Bortier
Rue Saint-Jean

100 m

L'îlot Sacré

Guided by the crowds of tourists you'll have no trouble finding the truly magnificent Grand-Place, a theatrical square filled with cafés. Once you've got over your wonder, try exploring the narrow streets of the Îlot Sacré (Sacred Island), avoiding such hazards as the restaurants in Rue des Bouchers and the souvenir shops on the way to Mannekenpis. The luxury stores, secondhand booksellers and friendly cafés are just around the corner, but don't go on a Sunday, because everything is shut.

❶ Grand-Place★★★
See Don't Miss p. 66.

The inhabitants of Brussels have a taste for individualism and eclecticism, as shown by this magnificent group of corporation houses, rebuilt after the French bombardment of 1695. Flemish Italian-Spanish in style, the façades are crumbling under their baroque decorations and

Detail of the façade of the Town Hall in Grand-Place

gilding. The 'richest theater in the world' (according to French writer Jean Cocteau) is home to a bird market on Sunday mornings and a magnificent revival of bygone splendor during the annual Ommegang festival, a re-enactment of the Joyous Entry of Emperor Charles V in 1549.

❷ Town Hall★★★

Grand-Place
See Don't Miss p. 66
☎ **02 279 43 65**
Guided tours (25 pers. max.): Tue. and Wed. 2.30pm, 1 Apr.-30 Sep. also Sun. at 10.45am; arrive 30 min in advance. Entrance charge.

Interior of the Town Hall

The only Gothic building on the square (the king's house opposite is a 19th-century

pastiche), it was built in two stages, giving rise to a legend that the architect threw himself off the tower when he saw that the two wings were asymmetrical. St Michael, patron saint of the city, slays the dragon at the top of the carved stone steeple. Inside are some of the fine 17th- and 18th-century tapestries that made the reputation of the Brussels weavers.

❸ Église Saint-Nicolas★★

Rue au Beurre
☎ **02 513 80 22**
Mon.-Fri. 10-12am and 4-6pm, Sat. 10-12am Entrance free.

Along with the city hall this church, dedicated to the patron saint of merchants, with little houses clinging to its sides, is one of the few remnants of the Middle Ages. The butter market used to be held in front of it. The church is Gothic in style, with fine paneling and Louis XIV pews. Take a look at the *Virgin and Sleeping Child*, attributed to Rubens, on the left-hand pillar in front of the choir, and a cannonball buried in the stone, which is a reminder of the fighting in 1695.

❹ Dandoy biscuit factory★★

31, rue au Beurre
☎ **02 511 03 26**
Mon.-Sat. 8.30am-6.30pm Sun. and holidays 10.30am-6.30pm.

A shop smelling wonderfully of cinnamon, almond and butter. In this 17th-century house five generations of Dandoys have been making *speculoos, pain à la grecque* (see p. 41), almond bread and marzipan cake flavored with orange flower since 1829. Food

lovers will be unable to resist, especially as the *speculoos* come in the shape of St Nicholas or a pot-bellied burgher.

❺ À la Bécasse★

11, rue de Tabora
☎ **02 511 00 06**
Every day 10am-1pm (2pm Fri.-Sat.).

If you fancy a glass of good *lambic* served with bread and cream cheese, hidden away at the end of this cul-de-sac you'll find this café, full of gleaming copper kegs. It's been here since 1877 and is one of the last establishments that still sells draught *lambic* and *kriek*. Two varieties of lambic, *doux*

☎ 02 217 27 53
www.toone.be
Reservations on
☎ 02 511 71 37
**Performances at 8.30pm
Tue. to Sat.**

For an unusual experience how about *El Cid*, *Othello* or *The Three Musketeers* performed in the Brussels dialect by puppets? These shows have been running for 170 years. Like Woltje, emcee Toone VII, alias José Géal, has all the characteristic arrogance and rebellious spirit of the true *Brusseleir*. The show continues in the café next door.

(sweet) or *blanc* (white), are served in stoneware jugs and it's renowned for being a potent brew!

two restaurants worthy of the name in this district, the *Ogenblik* and the *Taverne du Passage*.

❻ La Bourse★

Place de la Bourse.

Built by Léon Suys (1873) on the site of the Des Récollets convent, this is one of the key buildings in the Anspach city plan. Its façade looks like a Roman temple weighed down with baroque decorations, reflecting the wealth of a young and rapidly growing nation. The sculptors whose work decorates the building include the young Rodin, who is supposed to have contributed to the allegorical groups of *Asia* and *Africa*.

❼ Galeries royales Saint-Hubert★★★

**See Don't Miss p. 66
Access via rue du Marché-aux-Herbes.**

Since it opened in 1847 the city's most elegant passage has been a meeting-place for Brussels' high society. Housed between the pilasters under its vast glass roof are huge apartments, concert halls, luxury stores, antique shops and the only

❽ Théâtre Toone★★

6, impasse Schuddeveld (access via the small rue des Bouchers)

❾ Tropismes★★

**11, galerie des Princes
☎ 02 512 88 52
Sun.-Mon. 1.30-6.30pm,
Tue.-Thu. 10am-6.30pm,
Fri. 10am-8pm,
Sat. 10.30am-6.30pm.**

A 19th-century cabaret venue, all gold, stucco, columns and mirrors, is now home to one of the city's largest bookshops, specializing in literature and the social sciences. Literary gatherings are held here, maintaining Brussels' traditional role as an intellectual center, which it acquired when French writers Victor Hugo and Charles Baudelaire were in exile here.

The puppets of Théâtre Toone

⑩ Manufacture belge de dentelles★

6-8, galerie de la Reine,
☎ 02 511 44 77
Mon.-Sat. 9.30am-6pm,
Sun. 10am-4pm (closed
Sun. in Nov. and Feb.).

If you like lace make sure you step inside this venerable shop which has been supplying Brussels' high society with wedding veils and christening gowns since 1810. Here, depending on how much you want to pay, you can buy lace that's either entirely hand-made, or hand-stitched on a machine-produced template. It's also worth asking to see their special collection.

⑪ À la mort subite★

7, rue Montagne-aux-
Herbes-Potagères
☎ 02 513 13 18
Mon.-Sat. 11am-1am,
Fri.-Sat. 11am-2am,
Sun. 1pm-1am.

This long café, with its walls stained by generations of smokers is a Brussels institution, where you can sample a generous gueuze beer known as *Mort Subite* or 'Sudden Death'. If you're a

beer connoisseur, why not order a *Faro*, a one-year-old lambic sweetened with candy sugar and caramel.

⑫ La courte échelle★

12, rue des Éperonniers
☎ 02 512 47 59
Every day except Wed. and
Sun., 11.30am-1.30pm and
2-6pm.

This is a paradise for Lilliputians. There are houses just their size and everything that goes inside, from furniture to food and the china to eat it from. Items include crystal chandeliers, oriental carpets, toys, a

goldfish bowl; in other words the whole world in miniature, which will fascinate young and old alike. There's absolutely everything you could ever imagine, including corsets for the little ladies.

⑬ Galerie Bortier★★

Access rue de la Madeleine
Tue.-Sat. 10am-6.30pm.

At rue de la Madeleine end, this narrow covered passage has a façade in the Flemish baroque style and is decorated inside with cast-iron ornaments. This is a world of muffled quiet, where serious collectors of old books and engravings mingle with ordinary browsers looking for a secondhand paperback.

⑭ Plaizier★★

50, rue des Éperonniers
☎ 02 513 47 30
Mon.-Sat. 11am-6pm.

Here you can treat yourself to a fascinating series of 1930s views of Brussels in the rain, a *hecho en Mexico* diary, a miniature reproduction of Hoffmann's *Sitzmachine*, a dictionary of pictograms for serious travelers, or even that great book by Dr Alan Francis *Sex after 50*!

PAIN À LA GRECQUE, A BRUSSELS SPECIALITY

'Greek-style bread' is a strange name for the lightly-sugared biscuits that have been made in Brussels since the 16th century! In fact the recipe didn't come from the Greeks but from the monks of Fossé aux Loups and originally consisted of a long sugar-coated loaf eaten on feast days. The name *Bruut van de grecht* must have been too hard to pronounce for the French soldiers who occupied the city in the 17th century. They called it *pain à la grecque*, but the recipe has stayed the same.

2

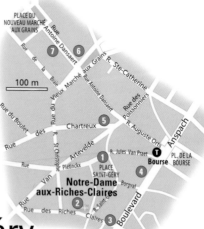

PLACE DU
NOUVEAU MARCHÉ
AUX GRAINS

Rue Antoine Dansaert

Rue de la Braie

7

6

R. Ste-Catherine

Rue du Vieux Marché aux Grains

Rue Antoine Dansaert

Rue des Poissonniers

Rue du Boulet

des

Chartreux

5

R. Auguste Orts

Anspach

Rue

Rue

Artevelde

St-Christophe

Pletinckx

R. Jules Van Praet

1

Bourse

T

PL. DE LA
BOURSE

PLACE
SAINT-GÉRY

4

Van

Notre-Dame
aux-Riches-Claires

Borgval

Rue

des

Riches

2

R. Saint-

Claires

3

Boulevard

100 m

Saint-Géry,
birthplace of the city

It was here that *Bruocsella* ('the house in the marsh') was founded in 979, when Charles of France built an oratory dedicated to St Géry on a small island in the Senne covered in wild irises. This district suffered badly from the greed of property developers around the 1970s, but is now gradually being revived thanks to the dynamism of its inhabitants, who have turned it into the trendiest place in central Brussels. Along with the gay clubs you'll find shops selling avant-garde fashions by Belgian designers and restaurants and cafés with wild and wacky interiors.

❶ Place Saint-Géry★★

The hour of revenge has come for St Géry. Although his church, now buried under the great hall of the meat market (1881), will never see the light of day again, the square dedicated to him is once more a popular and thriving area.

On the cymas, or cornices, of the Saint-Géry covered market, one can read the history of a district whose heart beats mainly at night.

❷ Notre-Dame-aux-Riches-Claires★

**23, rue des Riches-Claires
☎ 02 511 09 37
Sat. 3-6pm,
Sun. 9.30am-1.30pm.
Entrance free.**

A fine example of the architecture of the Flemish Renaissance (1665), the church of the St Clare nuns with its huge hemispherical

dome has strange gables with decorative scrolls over the ends of the transept and choir. During restoration works after the fire of 1989, remains were uncovered dating back to the Roman period.

❸ Man to Man★

11, rue des Riches-Claires
☎ **02 514 02 96**
Tue.-Fri. 10am-6.30pm,
Sat. 10am-6pm.

Ladies, don't bother stepping into this hairdresser's if you want a perm. Apart from the whips and nipple clamps, all the S&M accessories on display in the window are for men only, unless you go in for latex G-strings and leather chaps. As for the boys, we'd better warn you that crew cuts are the house specialty.

❻ RUE ANTOINE-DANSAERT: DOWN TOWN BRUSSELS

It's in this street with its working-class 18th-century houses that the fashionable Belgian avant-garde has decided to establish itself. Minimalist stores coexist with restaurants with baroque decor where eating well is not necessarily the first priority of the clientele who frequent them.

❹ Au Suisse★★★

73-75, boulevard Anspach
☎ **02 512 95 89**
Mon.-Fri. 10am-6pm,
Sat. 10am-7pm.

Feeling a little hungry? Stop at Au Suisse, the sandwich and surprise-loaf caterer. He has catered for all the buffets of famous parties. The place has existed for 150 years and you'll be able to savor, at the bar, lovely salads, hot soups, home-made pastries or delicious sandwiches made with 'French bread' (the baguette) for about €2.80!

❺ Le Greenwich★★

7, rue des Chartreux
☎ **02 511 41 67**
Every day 11am-2am.

This café has hardly changed at all since it opened at the end of the 19th century with its dark paneling, marble tables, glass roof and an old National cash register. The interior has inspired many film-makers, including Delvaux, and regulars once included the painter Magritte, who was a fanatical chess-player. Although it's lively in the evenings, the hushed atmosphere in the afternoons is the perfect aid to concentration and the chess players are mostly on sparkling water. But there's nothing to stop you ordering a glass of Trappiste.

❼ Stijl★★★

74, rue Antoine-Dansaert
☎ **02 512 03 13**
Mon.-Sat. 10.30am-6.30pm.

This great shop, the showcase for the Antwerp designers (Ann Demeulemeester, Dries Van Noten, Dirk Bikkembergs and Raf Simons) and natives of Brussels (Xavier Delcour), has livened up the district all by itself. Very trendy clothing for men and women, exclusive, expensive, but very good quality. Their main mission is to seek out new and original designer talent.

3

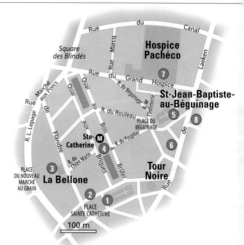

Square des Blindés

Hospice Pachéco

Rue du Canal

Laeken

Rue Marcq

Rue du Grand Hospice

R. du Béguinage

Marché aux Porcs

Quai

Rue R. L. Lepage

Quai au de Flandre

R. du Rouleau

St-Jean-Baptiste-au-Béguinage

5

8

PLACE DU BÉGUINAGE

Ste-Catherine

M

4

R. du Chien Marin

aux Briques

R. du Peuplier

6

PLACE DU NOUVEAU MARCHÉ AU GRAIN

3 La Bellone

Brüder

Tour Noire

Rue

2

1

PLACE SAINTE CATHERINE

100 m

Sainte-Catherine,
the old waterfront area

Early-risers mingle with night-owls amid the choreographed comings and goings of trucks loaded with fish. Although the area of the river port has been filled in for decades, and the fish markets have all been bulldozed, most of the locals are still engaged in the seafood trade. This area is particularly pleasant on fine days, when the pavements are covered with tables and chairs and musicians give impromptu concerts.

❶ Place Sainte-Catherine★

The lovely gabled façades and trees shading the square almost make you forget the heavy forms of its 'neo-Gothic-Renaissance' church. Stop off at Martine's to taste the *moules* or sample the wares of the mussel-sellers, which the locals eat with bread and butter (from mid-July to mid-April Mon.-Sat. 9.30am-5.30pm).

❷ La Belle Maraîchère★★

11A, place Sainte-Catherine
☎ 02 512 97 59
Fri.-Tue. 12am-2.30pm
and 6pm-9.30pm.

Easily the best value for money in the area. For 40 years Freddy Devreker has been delighting his customers' tastebuds with dishes that skillfully combine fish and shellfish. Terrine of ray and

crab, scallops with *Noilly Prat*, superb fish soup and grilled turbot with hop shoots when they're in season. The desserts are just as delicious and you'll be given a very warm welcome.

❸ La Bellone★★★

46, rue de Flandre
☎ 02 513 33 33
www.bellone.be
Tue.-Fri. 10am-6pm
Entrance free.

Step through the porch and you'll discover a little gem in the baroque style. This splendid patrician house dates from 1697 and is dedicated to Bellona, the Roman goddess of war. In 1980 the building became a venue for performances and is also a place for meetings and discussions. It has a reference library, and sometimes performances are staged in the courtyard.

❹ Old fish market★

Also known as *Vismet*, this group of pools is all that remains of the river port, which was abandoned in the 19th century. The fish market hall (1883), a magnificent construction of cast iron and glass, was demolished in 1955 as the result of an absurd decision on the part of the authorities. The fish market is now held (4am-1pm) in the wholesalers' warehouses that line the old waterfront. Take a look at the lovely gabled houses, particularly Le Cheval Marin.

❺ Saint-Jean-Baptiste-au-Béguinage★★★

Place du Béguinage
☎ 02 217 87 42
Every day 10am-5pm
Entrance free.

This is one of those magical places where time seems to have stood still. The church, which dates from 1676, is a gem of Flemish Baroque and the narrow streets laid out in a star shape around it offer a haven of peace. Inside the church you'll find paintings in the style of Caravaggio by Van Loon, confession boxes guarded by angels and a stunning 18th-century pulpit dedicated to St Dominic.

❻ La Tentation★★

28, rue de Laeken
☎ 02 223 22 75
www.latentation.org
Mon.-Fri. 10.30am-midnight, Sat.-Sun. 6pm-midnight
A member's card (€8) gives you the right to reduced-price or free concerts.

It is the Spanish Celts who restored this splendid shop which originally sold fabric. Among the wrought-iron columns, a restaurant offers Iberian dishes on the mezzanine, whereas downstairs, on some evenings in the week, you can hear concerts of Galician or world music. Don't hesitate to ask for the *queimada*, a magic potion concocted by the house druid!

❼ Hospice Pachéco★★

7, rue du Grand-Hospice
☎ 02 218 69 32
Vis. de la chapelle
Sun. 9-12am or by arrangement. Entrance free.

The gardens of the Béguinage behind the church have given way to a fine group of neo-Classical buildings by Henri Partoes (1824). The hospice is still open and is laid out around two courtyards lined with arcades. Entrance is on Sunday morning or by request and you can visit the first courtyard and the circular chapel with its coffered dome.

❽ DROGUERIE LE LION★★

Pure poetry – a wonderful combination of sights and fragrances. The great glass jars contain pigments of every color, from burnt umber to scarlet, while the treasures hidden away in the wooden drawers include centaury flowers, artemisia and oregano. Mme Billet is always at the counter ready to give you her help and advice.

55, rue de Laeken
☎ 02 217 42 02; Mon.-Fri. 8.30am-5.30pm, Sat. 10am-4pm.

4

Place de Brouckère,
Brussels of the Belle Époque

It was a 19th-century dream of bringing magnificence to Brussels that led
to the burial of the Senne river and the transformation of a working-class
neighborhood into a Parisian-style boulevard. In those days Place de
Brouckère was frequented by the new bourgeoisie, who dined at the
Métropole after the theater. Today it's caught between two opposing forces:
popular culture is invading from the north, while to the south the luxury
shops are slowly returning, trying to restore the area's former glory. If you
look above the neon signs you'll certainly see some stunning façades.

❶ Place de Brouckère✶

In the days when it boasted
expensive cafés, brasseries,
grand hotels, theaters and the
first movie theater, this was one
of the city's most fashionable
areas. The construction of two
'American-style' towers in 1967
destroyed the harmony of the
square, leaving the way open to
an anarchic invasion of cutprice
stores. The recent renovation of
the art deco auditorium of the
Eldorado movie theater and the

Hôtel Métropole

refacing of some fine façades
may mean the long-awaited
revival is under way.

❷ Hôtel Métropole✶✶✶

31, place de Brouckère
☎ 02 217 23 00; Café 9am-
1am (2am Fri.-Sat.).

Nothing changes this grand
hotel. The passing of the years
and of several crowned heads
haven't left a mark on it. The
café terrace is always full,
summer and winter, while a
nostalgic feel to the Belle

Époque lounges is reminiscent of the Orient Express.

❸ Passage du Nord★

1, boulevard Adolphe-Max

At the beginning of the old Boulevard du Nord is a passage (1881) decorated with caryatids – columns in the shape of female figures. The architect was inspired by the motto on the lovely building next door, 'Hier ist den kater en de kat,' which won first prize for architecture in 1872. The exclusive shops have all moved out but oyster connoisseurs still

visit the Oyster Bar (Mon.-Sat. 11am-7pm ☎ 02 217 45 52) to enjoy Zeeland oysters at the counter, washed down with a glass of white wine.

❹ Rue Neuve★

A few mime artists perform to the crowds of stylish young people who rush from store to store and the heady smell of hot waffles is irresistible. This is

the busiest pedestrian street in Brussels, particularly on a Saturday. Here you can dress yourself cheaply from head to toe as long as you like T-shirts, bright colors and platform shoes.

❻ Théâtre de la Monnaie★★

**Place de la Monnaie
☎ 02 229 13 72; Sep.-May, guided tours Sat. at noon.**

Founded in 1700 this is Belgium's finest venue, hosting performances of work by Béjart and his 20th-century ballet from 1960 to 1989. It's a mixture of architectural styles: the façade dates from the Napoleonic era, the neo-baroque hall and royal box were designed by Pœlaert, while the foyer was decorated by two American conceptual artists, Sol LeWitt and Sam Francis.

❼ 100 % Design★

**30, boulevard Anspach
☎ 02 219 61 98
Tue.-Sat. 10am-6.30pm and Mon. 12am-6.30pm.**

This is the place to buy inflatable furniture and decorative items for your

home – if you've got the lungs to blow! In addition to the classic chairs and stools you'll find wastepaper baskets, photograph frames, clocks and even tulips full of air. There are floating fish to keep your water-bound little ones company and plastic Ron Arad shelving you can arrange any way you like, all at good prices.

❺ PLACE DES MARTYRS★★

This square of bourgeois residences built in the late 18th century in the purest neo-Classical style was one of the city's finest squares before becoming the sad symbol of linguistic quarreling. In the 1960s it was left to go to rack and ruin, before finally being renovated in the 'façadism' manner. On one side are the offices of the Flemish presidency, on the other the theater of the French-speaking community.

5

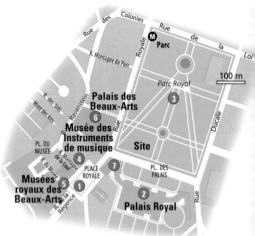

Coudenberg,
Mont des Arts

Coudenberg, located halfway between the upper and lower cities, has been a residence of princes since the 11th century. You may not be able to shop here, but you can fill up on culture in one of its four museums, catch a glimpse of the king or visiting celebrities, go for a jog round the park or listen to a concert at the Palais des Beaux-Arts. Best of all you'll get a superb view over Grand-Place from the top of the Mont des Arts.

❶ Place Royale★★★
See Don't Miss p. 69.

This elegant neo-Classical square, with its statue of Godefroi de Bouillon, is the work of Charles de Lorraine. Enter the arcade to the left of the Museum of Modern Art to explore the fine Louis XVI-style palace, whose wings close off the view of Museum Square.

❷ Palais Royal★★
See Don't Miss p. 69.

The Louis XVI façade, modified under Leopold II, hides two bourgeois residences built in the 18th century. The

building is very grand, but the king only comes here for official occasions.

❸ Parc Royal★
These lovely grounds, laid out in the French style over 13 ha/32 acres, were designed by

B. Guimard in 1775. As you walk along the tree-lined avenues you'll come upon a great many sculptures with mythological subjects, artificial lakes and delightful pavilions where concerts are staged in summer.

❹ Musée des Instruments de musique★★★

2, rue Montagne-de-la-Cour
☎ 02 545 01 30
www.mim.fgov.be
Tue., Wed., Fri. 9.30am-5pm; Thu. 9.30am-8pm (concert at 8pm);
Sat.-Sun.10am-5pm
See Don't Miss p. 67.

This art-nouveau building, created by Saintenoy in1899, houses one of the richest collections in the world, comprising more than 7,000 instruments including some very rare specimens invented by Adolphe Sax. Infrared headsets play music extracts to give you an idea of what these instruments sound like. Concerts on Thursday evenings.

❺ Musées royaux des Beaux-Arts★★★

3, rue de la Régence
☎ 02 508 32 11
www.fine-arts-museum.be
See p. 68 for practical information.
Entrance charge
See Don't Miss p. 68.

These museums offer a vast panorama of painting and sculpture in Belgium from the Middle Ages to recent times. Make sure you see the Flemish primitives, Brueghels and Rubens, in the period section. The underground gallery in the

Modern Art section (opened in 1984) is an architectural feat created by Bastin. Make sure you don't miss Spilliaert's sea paintings, the Flemish expressionists and the surrealist works by Delvaux and Magritte.

❻ Palais des Beaux-Arts★★★

23, rue Ravenstein
☎ 02 507 82 00
www.bozar.be

This Mecca of cultural life, now called Bozar after the great face-lift which gave it back its former luster, is one of the last realizations by Horta. It also houses a vast concert hall with remarkable acoustics, a theater, a well-stocked film library, exhibition rooms and a brasserie. In 1928, with its pure lines announcing art deco and above all a liberal use of concrete, it was looked on as a pioneer. Every year, the prestigious Queen Elizabeth Competition takes place here.

❼ Coundenberg archeological site★★

7, place des Palais (entrance via Bellevue Hotel)
☎ 02 545 08 00
www.musbellevue.be
See practical information p. 69 (guided tours: vigneron@kbs.frb.be)
Entrance charge
See Don't Miss p. 69.

Under the present Bellevue hotel, one of the most astonishing sites in Brussels is hidden: the former palace of the dukes of Brabant and Burgundy established in the 11th century. Destroyed by a violent fire in 1731, apparently due to the carelessness of the cooks too busy with cooking jams, the palace where Philippe le Bon and Charles V used to live was brought to light in 1995. Along a passage dug under Place Royale, via an impressive maze of streets and vestiges, one can reach the Aula Magna, the huge ceremonial hall of the dukes of Burgundy.

SUNDAY WITH THE ARTS

You need not be bored in Brussels on Sundays. A single ticket enables you to attend a Bozar concert (at 11am; come early to secure a seat), to go the former Brussels Palace, the Museum of Musical Instruments and the Fine Arts museums, not forgetting the temporary exhibitions and the children's workshops. The price of the pass is €11 at Bozartickets, 5 rue Ravenstein. Information on ☎ 05 507 84 32; www.montdesarts.be.

6

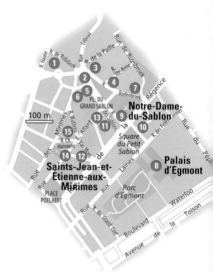

PL. DU GRAND SABLON

Notre-Dame-du-Sablon **⑨**

100 m

⑬ **⑪**

⑮

R. Ch. Hanssens

⑭ **⑫**

Square du Petit Sablon

⑩

Saints-Jean-et-Etienne-aux-Minimes

PLACE POELAERT

Parc d'Egmont

Palais d'Egmont **⑧**

Waterloo

Sablon,

a tour of the antiques shops

Sablon's streets are lined with the city's best antiques shops, its flea market is the busiest in Brussels and the terraces of its smart cafés are always crowded. An absolute must for your weekend, it's the place to catch the latest hits, get the name of the most fashionable clubs or taste some of Wittamer's incomparable cakes. And if it's antiques you're after, you'll find some fine things at quite reasonable prices.

❶ Marie Storms★★

13, rue de Rollebeek
☎ 02 511 73 14
Tue.-Sat. 10.30am-6pm.

If you've always dreamed of wearing the jewelry of Battista Sforza or Isabelle d'Este, step inside Marie Storms' superb store. Her inspiration comes from the Italian Renaissance and her glass beads from Murano. Powdered gold blown onto lapis lazuli, baroque strings of pearls, byzantine necklaces, antique cameos, in other words

jewels fit for a queen, at very reasonable prices. A favorite store of the Belgian upper classes, including Queen Paola.

❷ Place du Grand-Sablon★★

The magnificent 17th- and 18th-century façades set the scene for the antiques market

which is held here every
weekend (Sat. 9am-6pm and
Sun. 9am-2pm). Since the
wealthy Eurocrats arrived it's
been hard to unearth a
bargain here, but it's still a
great place to wander around.

Wittamer★★

12-13, place du Grand-Sablon
☎ 02 512 37 42
Mon. 10am-6pm, Tue.-Sat.
8am-7pm, Sun. 7am-6.30pm.

The home of delicious cakes,
good bread and Viennese
pastries since 1910, this shop is
so successful that Henri
Wittamer (the third) has also
opened a cake shop at no. 6.
You can either eat your *samba*
chocolate cake, meringue
soufflé with fresh fruit or
pouques aux raisins in the
shop or take out.

4 Impasse Saint-Jacques★

Wartevelle, n°8,
☎ 02 513 01 75 – Mon.- Sat.
10am-6pm, Sun. 10am-2pm.
Congo Gallery, n°2,
☎ 02 511 47 67 – Mon.-Sat.
11am-6pm.
Ambre Congo, n°17,
☎ 02 511 16 62 – Tue.-Fri.
10am-12.30pm and 2-6pm,
Sat. 11am-1pm, Sun. 3-6pm.

Though it has lost much of its
charm since the building of the
Jolly hotel, this *impasse* (cul-
de-sac) is still the haunt of
sellers of ethnic artifacts. Africa
is predominant with tribal
weaponry, wooden sculptures,
necklaces and terracotta objects.

5 The Art Home★★

10, place du Grand-Sablon
☎ 02 504 80 30
www.thearthome.be
Entrance free.

The magnificent private
mansion built in 1921 for the
furrier Mallien is the new
cultural pole of the Sablon,

where you can look at, buy and
savor art in all its forms. Besides
the exhibitions of antiques and
paintings organized every other
month by the Fine Arts auction
room, here you can find a very
attractive art bookshop, and a

restaurant room where you can
taste culinary creations. For
three prestigious international
shows, it becomes a meeting
place for the best antique
dealers (November), 20th
century antique dealers
(March) and dealers in
Primitive Arts (June). Do not
hesitate to step inside!

6 Chez Richard★★

2, rue des Minimes
☎ 02 512 14 06
Every day 7am-3am (5am
Fri.-Sat.).

It is in this old café, a former

haunt of postmen, with its decor
practically unchanged since
1948, that you can really feel
the heart of the Sablon beating.
Depending on the time of day,
you can meet antique dealers
talking business, students
having a late breakfast,
aficionados of black pudding
with stewed apples and home-
made *stoemp* and lovers of the
aperitif. Yet it is during the
weekend that the atmosphere is
the warmest. Oyster lovers, take
note: this is the place to sample
them from October to April, and
fans of French songs of the
1980s can dance on the tables!

7 Écailler du Palais Royal★★★

18, rue Bodenbroek
☎ 02 512 87 51
Open lunchtime and
evening, closed Sun.,
holidays and August.

Grand-Sablon market

Given two stars in the *Michelin Guide* this place has a cosy interior with blue mosaics, where you'll be served succulent dishes based on fish and shellfish. Besides dishes such as curried lobster ravioli and John Dory *au beurre blanc*, the *plat du jour* is always worth trying. Be prepared for a fairly large bill.

❽ Palais d'Egmont★★

Only the garden is open to the public (entrance rue du Grand-Cerf).

This magnificent 18th-century aristocratic residence, which closes off the view of Sablons, was home to the d'Egmont and d'Arenberg families before being turned over to the Ministry of Foreign Affairs. The garden contains two Ginkgo biloba trees and a tulip tree.

❾ Notre-Dame-du-Sablon★★★

6, rue Bodenbroeck
☎ 02 511 57 41
Mon.-Fri. 9am-6pm,
Sat.-Sun. 10am-6pm
Entrance free.

A small boat depicted above the south door is a reminder that in 1348 this was the mode of transport used to bring the miraculous statue of the Virgin Mary to the Church of the Crossbowmen's Guild. Unusually this jewel of the flamboyant Brabant Gothic style has internal flying buttresses. On November 3 a hunting horn calls the faithful to a special mass celebrating the feast day of St Hubert.

❿ Square du Petit-Sablon★

This is a delightful little park, full of flowers and lovely to walk in. In the center is a group sculpture showing Count d'Egmont and Count de Hornes, heroes of the resistance to the Spanish occupiers, with ten 16th-century humanists standing around them in a semi-circle. The statues of 48 16th-century guild masters are mounted on the iron railings around the park. See if you can identify them!

⓫ Philippe Denys★★★

1, rue des Sablons
☎ 02 512 36 07
Tue.-Fri. 10.30am-6.30pm,
Sat. 1.30-6.30pm, Sun.
11am-2pm.

Philippe Denys is a discoverer of things. His favorites are the European creations from the 1850s to the 1880s. Planished silverware of

Scandinavian or Italian design, old and contemporary jewelry, photographs by Man Ray, ceramics and furniture

---

SABLON FESTIVALS

In April, the festival of baroque music spreads to churches and antique stores throughout Brussels; in June, the Primitive Arts galleries organize Bruneaf, an exhibition of non-European arts; in July, the procession of the Ommegang starts from Notre-Dame Church; during the last weekend of November all the stores and galleries, lit up for the occasion, celebrate the 'Nights of Sablon' with champagne and concerts.

XXᵉ siècle déco-arts

are presented in this vast place where purity of line is given pride of place.

⑫ Yves Macaux★★★

43, rue de la Régence
☎ 02 502 31 16
Tue.-Fri. 2-6pm,
Sat. 11am-6pm.

Furniture with lines that are pure and straight, using simple materials and embodying a modernism before its time, in contrast to the exuberant creations of Victor Horta that were then all the rage. This is where you you'll find all the big names of the Viennese Secession: Adolphe Loos, Otto Wagner, Josef Hoffmann and Marcel Kammerer.

⑬ XXᵉ siècle déco-arts★★

12-14, rue Ernest Allard
☎ 02 513 40 42
Tue.-Sun. 10am-6pm.

For the collectors of unusual items from the 1940s to the 1970s: unique pieces of Scandinavian and Italian design, vintage furniture and abstract painting. Here you'll find what you are after at reasonable prices. Worth a special mention are the Italian lamps (Fontana Arte, Mazega), the furniture by Poul Kjaerholm, Arne Jacobsen and Poul Henningsen and the creations of Fornassetti. And who knows, maybe you'll allow yourself to be tempted by a desk from the Belgian designer, Jules Wabbes?

⑭ Église Saints-Jean-et-Étienne-aux-Minimes★★

62, rue des Minimes
☎ 02 511 93 84
Every day 10am-1pm
Mass at 11.30am and
12.15pm Sun.
Entrance free.

The Italian-style façade with its pilasters (1715) hints at the beautiful order and light of the classical interior. Besides the Gregorian chants sung during Sunday mass, the church regularly hosts concerts of music by Bach and Handel.

⑮ Le Perroquet★

31, rue Watteeu
☎ 02 512 99 22
Mon.-Sat. 11am-1am,
Sun.-Tue. 11am- 12.30am.

Inside you'll find chequered floor tiles, stained glass, gently filtered light and a carved wooden counter. Outside, the pavement tables are seized as soon as the first ray of sunlight appears. At any time you'll find an enormous choice of pitas and a few healthy salads. You can also enjoy a glass of wine in this lovely art-nouveau bistro.

7

**Notre-Dame-
de-la-Chapelle**

Marolles,
a working-class area

In contrast to aristocratic Sablon, Marolles' narrow streets and cul-de-sacs have always been home to a multicultural society. A mix of artisans, outlaws and immigrants from around the world has produced the typical Marollian: a rebellious joker, speaking a dialect of French mixed with Flemish. Here the junk trade has been going on for years and markets are still held every day on the square. Make sure you visit this engaging district, which is fast disappearing. After the property developers, it's now the restaurants and clubs that are moving in.

❶ Place du Jeu-de-Balle★★★

Second-hand market every day 7am-2pm.

At 5am enormous piles of disparate objects are unpacked and swooped on by collectors. Amongst the rubbish you can sometimes unearth a real bargain. On Sundays they take more care over the presentation, and the prices rise accordingly. The best time for bargain hunters is on Tuesdays or early Friday morning, but it's

entertaining at any time to catch the Brussels *zwanze* and watch deals being struck in Arabic.

❷ Chez Marcel★★★

20, place du Jeu-de-Balle
☎ 02 511 13 75
**Every day 8am-6.30pm
(closed 25 Dec.)**

One of the last authentic cafés in Marolles where *zinnekes* and tourists sit elbow-to-elbow to knock back a lager or lap up, at all hours of the day, one of

Marcel's famous soups – especially the 'machinegun soup' (with beans!). Other house specialties are *pottekeis*, *tartine* (bread roll) with white cheese and onion and the superb 'grandmother's omelette', not to mention Marcel's whiskers, the Marollian sense of humor and the pre-war decor. A must!

❸ Cité Reine-Astrid★

When they were built in 1914 these apartment blocks, arranged in six parallel rows, were at the cutting edge of avant-garde social housing. Hygiene, light and functionality were the watchwords of the builders of these colored brick constructions, now mainly inhabited by people of North African origin, who have lent

their own personal character to the buildings.

❹ Antoni Jassogne★★

21, rue des Renards
☎ 02 511 85 14
Mon.-Sat. 10.30am-6.30pm.

Pause for an moment to admire the precise workmanship of these stringed instruments. Take in the subtle aroma of maple and spruce, the tools with polished handles on the bench

and the violins waiting to be played. A violin made here costs around €10,000.

❺ Easy Tempo★★

146, rue Haute
☎ 02 513 54 40
Tue.-Sat. 12-2.30pm/6.30-10.30pm, Sun. 12-2.30pm.

If the Belle-Epoque tiles call to mind the former occupation of this baker and pastrycook, now it is aromas of tomato, garlic and *tartufo* which waft from this place devoted to *la dolce vita* and *la cucina casalinga*. Delicious pasta, such as *strozzapreti*, Sicilian-style pizzas and selections from the market, with a fine choice of Italian wines. Cosmopolitan clientele and a perfect welcome by Sebastiano and Benedetto. It is advisable to reserve beforehand.

❼ Apostrophe★★★

50, rue Blaes;
☎ 02 502 67 38

www.apostrophe1.com
Mon.-Sat. 10am-6pm,
Sun. 10am-4pm.

This is the meeting place of curious travelers and collectors of bizarre objects. The shop specializes in old trade furniture (from 1880 to 1930) and unusual objects, from a grocery counter to rows of office drawers and pharmacy cupboards. The prices are as attractive as the reception is welcoming.

❽ Notre-Dame-de-la-Chapelle★★

Place de la Chapelle
☎ 02 512 21 40
9am-5pm Jun-Sep.;
12.30am-4.30pm Oct.-May

A strange baroque tower rises above the old parish of the painter Brueghel the Elder, who's buried here. The 13th-century Romano-Gothic core has been extended over the years, but this in no way mars one of the city's most beautiful churches.

❻ RUE HAUTE, RUE BLAES★★

Right by the court of justice, these two streets, always busy and lively, harbor an incredible number of antique dealers, decoration stores and secondhand dealers. To make good bargains, go into Passage 125 Blaes (p.125) or into l'Espace 161 (161 rue Haute) which contain scores of exhibitors, with furniture and objects of all styles, and where prices are displayed. You can then haggle at your leisure!

8

Avenue
R. Charleroi
R. Berckmans
Rue Blanche
Rue de Florence
Hôtel Otlet ⑪
⑬ Rue de Veydt
de
Rue
Rue
Defacqz
Hôtel Tassel ⑩
200 m
Faider ⑫ R. Paul-Emile Janson
Rue
R. de l'Amazone
⑦ ⑧ Livourne
⑥ du
Bailli
Louise
Rue du Châtelain
R. A. Campenhout
Washington
R. du Magistrat
Rue
PARVIS DE LA TRINITÉ
⑤
Rue
PLACE DU CHÂTELAIN
Chaussée
Rue
② Rue Africaine
⑨
de
l'Aqueduc
③
Musée Horta
Rue de Tabellion
R. Fourmois
Rue du Page
①
Mail
Américaine
Chaussée
de
Rue
R. du Prévôt
Waterloo
⑭

Ixelles
and Saint-Gilles,
the art-nouveau manifesto

This is an elegant business district, with a great number of art-nouveau houses. This anti-rational, exuberant style, thought shocking when the houses were built, was adopted by the new bourgeois industrialists, who commissioned the best architects to build their residences. Today their sensuous façades conceal offices and a few good restaurants; but if you really want to plunge into the world of the visionary art-nouveau architect Horta, make sure you go on a tour of his private house. The area is liveliest on Wednesday afternoons, market day on place du Châtelain.

❶ La Quincaillerie★★★

45, rue du Page
☎ 02 538 25 53
Every day except Sat. and Sun. lunchtime.

Wooden drawers from floor to ceiling, a *Temps Modernes* clock and wrought iron characterize this former art-nouveau hardware store, now a brasserie. All the food is

made with fresh ingredients, style and skill. Choose from fresh oysters or special dishes, divine home-made desserts and a good wine list. All the staff are women, and the diners tend to be lawyers and people in fashion or advertising.

❷ Musée Horta★★★

25, rue Américaine
☎ 02 543 04 90

www.hortamuseum.be
Tue.-Sun. 2-5.30pm
(closed 1 Jan., 1 May, 1 and
11 Nov., 25 Dec.)
Entrance charge.

The Horta museum is located
in the private house and
workshop of this architect of
genius. Built between 1898 and
1901, it exemplifies the height
of the art nouveau movement.
Besides a spectacular staircase
crowned by a bronze-colored
glass roof, the dwelling has
kept a large part of its interior
design, mosaics, stained-glass
windows, furniture and wall
paintings.

❸ W80★★

80, rue de Washington
☎ 02 642 97 67
Mon.-Sat. 11am-6.30pm.

This is a novelty shop *par
excellence*. On the tables and
shelves there are unusual
items made by well-known or
less well-known designers.
Watch the cosmo-jetz robots or
the mosquitoes which can
perform somersaults. Things
for the home, accessories for
men and women, gifts to be
admired, touched, listened to,
tasted or smelled.

❹ Mais il est où le soleil ?★★★

38, place du Châtelain
☎ 02 538 82 77

Mon. 2-6.30pm,
Tue.-Sat.11am-6.30pm.

A shop where you can be sure
to find an item of clothing
which is both comfortable and
becoming, whether you are
skinny or well-rounded. It is
in India that Valérie Pollet,
the Brussels designer, finds
her inspiration and her
materials – cotton, linen,
silk and viscose – and the
ultra-feminine color of her
clothes. With layering, you
can create very original
outfits (about €170) by using
transparency, and length,
and matching pieces and
accessories for different
seasons as you please.
Moreover, the sales assistants
are very good at advising you.

❺ Lune après lune★★

102, rue du Bailli
☎ 02 538 63 26
Mon. 2-6.30pm,
Tue.-Sat. 10.30am-6.30pm.

Strings of flowery fairy lights,
beautiful fashion jewelry,
papier-mâché chandeliers,
mirrors for women with full
figures, kitsch trolleys, diva
gloves for the washing up,
'cow' alarm-clocks, to name
but a few – the ideas for
gifts and ornaments are
innumerable! The two friends
who own this shop favor small
craftsmen and original objects.
To please somebody or just
yourself, from €5.

❻ Eva Luna★★★

41, rue du Bailli
☎ 02 647 46 45
Mon.-Sat. 10.30am-6.30pm.

Ladies, here is the sensuous
place you have always dreamt
of! Intimate atmosphere and
the help of three specialists to
guide your choice from the
vast range of products and
accessories that will make you

more attractive, arouse your senses and give you pleasure. Natural beauty-care creams, delicate massage oils, suggestive and refined underwear, erotic accessories – the opportunities for extravagance are endless. Of course, men are also welcome!

7 La Septième Tasse★

37, rue du Bailli
☎ 02 647 19 71
www.7etasse.com
Tue.-Sat. 11am-7pm.

Plain or flavored teas, green or black teas, semi-fermented teas, in total more than 160 varieties. In this tea shop you'll find out everything about this divine drink. You'll get explanations about the tastes, the origins and you'll discover a world of immeasurable wealth. You can also buy high-class teapots or cups of British, Japanese or Belgian design.

8 Le Framboisier doré★★

35, rue du Bailli
☎ 02 647 51 44
May to mid-Sep., Tue.-Sun. 11.30am-11pm; mid-Sep. to Apr., Wed.-Sun. 11.30am-7pm.

Fresh milk, eggs, vanilla pods and fruit are combined to make wonderful old-fashioned ice cream. The ice-cream maker's creative imagination will take you down uncharted paths. From flowers to Sauternes and gueuze, there are 200 flavors to try in this pretty café which also serves waffles, cakes and hot chocolate.

9 Peinture fraîche★★

10, rue du Tabellion
☎ 02 537 11 05
Tue.-Sat. 11am-7pm.

Established in the square in front of Trinité church for over 10 years, this friendly little bookshop specializes in 20th-century architecture, photography, graphic design and fine art. The shelves are full of enticing books and you'll always get a warm welcome.

10 Hôtel Tassel★

6, rue Paul-Émile Janson.
A glass bow window set in metal and yellow stone, in continuous, flowing lines, with small columns bursting out of the stone and a curving balustrade. All the themes of Horta's architectural language can be seen here, in his second design for a private residence (1893), created for his friend Professor Tassel.

11 Hôtel Otlet★

48, rue de Livourne.
The abandonment of symmetry in favor of a clever interplay of lines moving inwards and outwards reflects Octave Van Rysselberghe's desire to fit into the art nouveau movement. Comparing this building with the Hôtel Tassel, built at the same time, you sense a certain timidity on the architect's part, though his building is still elegant.

⑫ Ciamberlani and Janssens houses★★

48-50, rue Defacqz.
These two very different buildings (1897-98) designed by Paul Hankar have an impressive sobriety unusual in art-nouveau design. Hankar exploited the ornamental possibilities of combining brick, stone and multi-colored sgraffiti. Note the horseshoe openings, which are the trademark of Hankar.

⑬ L'Amadeus ★★

13, rue Veydt
☎ 02 538 34 27
Restaurant : Mon.-Sat.
6.30pm-midnight, Sun.
10am-2pm and 6.30pm-
midnight, closed 1 Jan.-8
Jan. and 15 Jul.-15 Aug.
Bar: Tue.-Sat. 6.30pm-
1.30am.
Minerva in the Tuscan blue yard, a pensive Medici in the black workshop, a lounge with mirrors and scores of candlesticks which light up at nightfall. A romantic setting fit for a movie, where you can sip grape nectars while classical music plays in the background. Terrestrial foods are not up to the prices

displayed but as long as you are intoxicated…

"Divine and primeval order no longer existed. A complete and different universe emerged from the shade where new and still irresolute rhythms mingled their strength and their infinite waves."
Émile Verhaeren.
Les Rythmes souverains, 1910.

⑭ Parc Tenbosch★★

Entrance in place Leemans
8am-9pm summer
and 8am-6pm winter.

Tenbosch Park, laid out in the 19th century, is a botanical garden marvelously richly planted and full of charm. Besides its innumerable rare plants, among which is the 'handkerchief tree' native to

China and its turtles in the ponds, the distinctive feature is a colony of wild budgerigars! They have taken up residence in a tree on the right hand side of the entrance. If they are still there, in order to find them let yourself be guided by their noise.

SGRAFFITI

Sgraffiti, which were very fashionable in the late 19th century to decorate art-nouveau façades, are wall decorations taken from the Italian Renaissance. A pale-colored wash is applied over a mix of mortar and ash, and then carved with ornamental designs and figures. Artists often drew the designs onto paper first, then transferred them to the façade by means of a toothed tracing wheel. Unlike frescos, the colors of sgraffiti are applied in several layers.

9

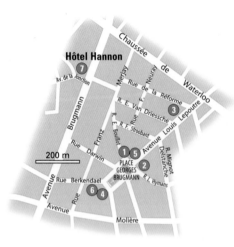

Hôtel Hannon ⑦

Chaussée de Waterloo

Av. de la Jonction

Merlay

Rue de la Réforme

R. E. Van Driessche

R. E. R. F. Stroobant

R. E. R. F. Bouillot

Rue Franz Darwin

Brugmann

Avenue Louis Lepoutre

③

200 m

① ⑤ PLACE GEORGES BRUGMANN ②

R. Mignot Dessanche

R. L. Hymans

Avenue Rue Berkendael

⑥ ④

Avenue

Molière

Place Brugmann,
the 'Paris' of Brussels

Take the number 60 bus and explore the beautiful avenues lined with trees and smart houses in Parisian and art-nouveau styles. This is village Brussels, where everyone knows everyone else and all are keen to achieve the good life. All the best stores for the home, clothes, flowers and antiques are here. Stop off for refreshment at a little restaurant or milk bar and, with most shops open on Sunday, what more could you ask for?

❶ Scènes de Ménage★★★

4, place Brugmann
☎ 02 344 32 95

Tue.-Sat. 10.30am-6.30pm, Mon. 2-6.30pm.

It's a real feat in this cramped space to create so many different ambiances for displaying various objects for the table and bathroom. Antique and modern are combined with impeccable taste. The place to find a horn caviar spoon, toothpicks with

a shell decoration or mock Victorian goblets.

❷ Catleya★★

118, avenue Louis Lepoutre
☎ 02 344 63 64
Mon.-Sat. 10am-8pm.

t's impossible not to be
attracted by the delicate leaves
and rustic bouquets over-
lowing from this shop onto
he pavement. The florist will
make up a Van Gogh or Manet
bouquet for you or, if you
prefer, will create one specially
n an earthenware pot, which
will fill your home with
fragrance as it dries.

③ Jacques Smadja★★

1, avenue Louis Lepoutre
☎ 02 346 50 13
Mon.-Sat. 11am-6.30pm.

A modern store where men and
women can get 'extravagant
classical' clothes. You'd like to
have a show-biz or an *avant-
garde* look? No problem;
Jacques Smadja has selected the
trademarks Paul Smith, N.Y.
Industriel or Joseph. Bold yet
wearable clothes.

④ Le Balmoral★★

21, place Brugmann
☎ 02 347 08 82
Tue.-Sun. 9am-8pm
(10.30pm Fri.).

A real 1960s milk bar with
pin-ups from the silver screen
and an American menu. Club
sandwiches, salads with a
choice of four different
dressings, home-made burgers,
cheesecake, brownies, cookies
and all kinds of milkshakes are
on the menu. Perfect for a late
breakfast with pancakes, as you
can eat here any time. Children
are welcome, with bibs and
baby food all part of the service.

⑤ Petrusse★★

109, avenue Louis Lepoutre
☎ 02 343 93 18
Mon.-Sat. 10.30am-6.30pm.

With a touch of her magic
wand, Isabelle de Forceville
makes ancient fabrics from
Kashmir live again. Using up-
to-the-minute shades, she
adapts these refined patterns to

shawls, stoles, woolen and
cotton scarves, but also to
home furnishings. You can
discover curtains, cushions
adorned with trimmings
but also a whole range of
accessories such as jewelry
with semiprecious stones,
and boxes.

⑥ Graphie sud★★★

195, rue Berkendael
☎ 02 344 31 92
Tue.-Sat. 11am-6.30pm,
Sun. 11.30am-3.30pm.

Surely the most beautiful
and inventive display in the
city. Violaine loves strange,
kitsch and surrealist objects,
thanksgiving plaques,
structured and comfortable
clothes, good chocolates,
conviviality and travel. This is
the perfect place to find a
personalized gift or the purse
of your dreams, to dress
yourself from head to toe or
buy a superb piece of jewelry.

⑦ L'HÔTEL HANNON★★★

One of the art-nouveau jewels built in 1903 by
Brunfaut for his friend Hannon, an engineer with a
passion for photography. The great symbolist fresco in
the staircase (Baudouin), the stained-glass windows
(Evaldre), the bas relief by Rousseau, the mosaic
ornamental tiles and the marbles selected by Gallé are

witnesses to the past
splendor of this mansion
which houses the
Contretype photographic
section. Retrospectives of
Hannon's work as a
photographer, a brilliant
representative of the
pictorialist movement,
are regularly organized
here in summer.

1, avenue de la Jonction
☎ 02 538 42 20
www.contretype.org
Mon.-Fri. 11am-6pm, Sat.-
Sun. 1-6pm (closed 1 Jan.,
1 May, 1 and 11 Nov.,
25 Dec.)
Entrance charge.

10

Cinquantenaire,
megalomania and museums

Leopold II had big ideas for celebrating his kingdom's jubilee: a triumphal arch, a park, an exhibition center and a wide avenue. This ambitious project was opened 25 years later and helped to create a district favored by the bourgeoisie, who settled here in magnificent private mansions. A century later they're now occupied by the Eurocrats who followed the bulldozers into the area. But while the stores here tend to be swanky and unexciting, it's worth visiting the museums in their leafy setting.

❶ Musées royaux d'Art et d'Histoire★★★

10, parc du Cinquantenaire
☎ 02 741 72 11
www.kmg-mrah.be
Tue.-Fri. 9.30am-5pm, Sat.,
Sun. and holidays 10am-5pm (closed 1 Jan., 1 May, 1 and 11 Nov., 25 Dec.)
Entrance charge
See Don't Miss p. 71.

You'll have to pick and choose from the vast collections in

Belgium's largest museum, a it contains objects from all around the world. Don't miss the great colonnade from Apameus, the *moai* from Easter Island, a magnificent Tupinamba cape of quetzal feathers and the god Chimù featured by Hergé in *Tintin and the Broken Ear*.

❷ Autoworld★★

11, parc du Cinquantenaire
☎ 02 736 41 65
www.autoworld.be
Every day 10am-6pm (Oct. Apr. 5pm; closed 25 Dec and 1 Jan). Entrance charg
See Don't Miss p. 70.

nder a great glass roof more
han 300 vehicles tell the story
f the automobile from its
onception to the 1950s.
ll countries are represented
y exceptional models,
ncluding Belgian-made cars
nd motorcycles. Gems
nclude King Albert I's
Minerva (1910), the first Ford
mobile home from 1924,
Gaston Lagaffe's Citroën and
F. Kennedy's Cadillac. Some
educed size models are on
ale in the shop!

Dédale★★

Galerie Cinquantenaire
☎ 02 734 22 55
Mon.-Sat. 10am-6.30pm.

t's playtime! Here you'll find
he widest possible choice of
rain-teasers, tarot cards, jigsaw
uzzles, board games, games
f strategy, everything for the
dult who wants to combine
musement with stimulation.
ou can play war games,
erform magic tricks or tell
ortunes for your friends.
However, you won't find any
lectronic games here, as
hey're banned.

❺ Aux Délices de Capoue★★★

36, avenue des Celtes
☎ 02 733 38 33
Every day noon-10pm.

People come from far and wide
to buy their home-made ice
cream here. Of the 40 flavors
available, make sure you try
speculoos and marzipan ice
cream, or a mandarin and
gooseberry sherbet. You can eat
in the clean, neat little tea
room, or take out.

❻ Maison Cauchie★★★

5, rue des Francs
☎ 02 673 15 06 or

❸ ATELIER DE MOULAGES (PLASTER CASTING)★★

Ever dreamed of having the Victory of Samothrace in
your living room? Well, there's a life-size plaster copy
of it in this studio hidden away in the museum
basement. In the highly surreal atmosphere created

by around 4,000 moulds,
they reproduce
masterpieces from the
neighboring museum as
well as from Florence,
Rome and Berlin. You'll
have to wait 6 weeks to
get one of these casts,
which are not on display

10, parc du Cinquantenaire
☎ 02 741 72 94
Tue.-Fri. 9.30am-noon
and 1.30-4pm,
Thu. 9.30am-6pm.
Entrance free.

☎ 02 733 86 84
Visits first weekend of the
month 11am-1pm and
2-6pm; Entrance charge.
See Don't Miss p. 72.

This former house-cum-studio
of the painter Paul Cauchie,
painstakingly renovated by the
De Cissys, illustrates another
side of art nouveau. Despite its
Japanese-style sgraffiti, the
pure lines of the façade are
close to Austrian secessionism
and to Mackintosh in design.
In the drawing room you can
see more sgraffiti and original
furniture.

❼ Maison Antoine★★

1, place Jourdan
☎ 02 230 54 56
Sun.-Thu. 11.30am-1am,
Fri.-Sat. 11.30am-2am.

It is on this square lined
with restaurants that you
can find the most famous
fritkot, or fries stall, in
Brussels which 'does not
advertise but serves the best
fries in Brussels and its
surroundings.' It has existed
for 50 years, and on the walls
are pinned the autographs
and photos of celebrities
such as Johnny Halliday,
Dave and Barzoti who came
here to enjoy the famous
cone of authentic fries.

11

Porte
de Namur

SQUARE
DU BASTION

Ⓜ Porte
de Namur

100 m

Chaussée   de   Wavre

Chaussée

Rue du Berger

Rue Francart

Rue St-Boniface

Rue Ernest Solvay

Rue de la Paix

Rue de la Longue Vie

Rue du Prince Royal

Rue d'Ixelles

Rue du Prince Albert

❶ ❻ ❽ ❷ ❸ ❼ ❺ ❹

Saint-
Boniface

Around Saint-Boniface

Between Matonge, which moves to African
rhythms, and the noisy Chaussée d'Ixelles,
with its stores selling cheap goods, there's a
little area that's been preserved. Here every
other house was designed by the art-nouveau
architect Ernest Blérot, who was active around
1900. Colored sgraffiti and fluid curves enliven
the façades. The atmosphere is warm and lively,
generated by a young population of students
from the Conservatoire and the cinema school.
The bookstores on Chaussée de Wavre are also
the favorite haunt of cartoon fans.

❶ Comptoir Florian★★

17, rue Saint-Boniface
☎ **02 513 91 03**
Tue.-Sat. 11am-8pm.

Proust would have loved this
little literary tea house in a
shop designed by Blérot in
1900. Here you can drink rare
blends or seasonal teas
flavored with green lemons

and bitter oranges in summer,
cinnamon and cloves in
winter. There's freshly ground
coffee, *pasteis* and homemade
cakes, a warm welcome and
a clientele of movie-lovers
and writers. Completely
non-smoking.

❷ Menus Propos★

22, rue Ernest Solvay
☎ **02 502 79 29**
Mon.-Sat. 11am-6.30pm.

Jamaican pepper, purple
mustard, savory honeys,
Espelette hot peppers, sweets
from the good old days…
this is an address for lovers of
rare spices and authentic
tastes. In this creative grocery
store Valérie Janssens, who
has cultivated a real passion
for cooking since her
childhood, will advise you on
the way to manipulate the
ingredients and reveal her
tricks and original recipes

L'Ultime Atome

such as the *sablé* (sugar-crust) pastry with *speculoos*.

❸ L'Ultime Atome★★

14, rue Saint-Boniface
☎ 02 511 13 67
Mon.-Thu. 8.30am-12.30am,
Fri.-Sat. 8.30am-1.30am,
Sun. 10am-12.30am.

A cafeteria not to be missed in this district where you can have a drink or eat tasty little dishes and salads at very reasonable prices (from €15 to €20). It is full of young and not so young people, aging hippies, artists, highbrows and yuppies; it is always crammed, trendy and very cosmopolitan. In the summer, the sidewalk is turned into a terrace.

❹ Église Saint-Boniface★

21, rue de la Paix
☎ 02 512 81 43
Mon.-Sat. 8.30am-5.30pm,
Sun. 8.30am-1pm
Entrance free.

Built in 1847 for parishioners tired of climbing the hill after attending mass in La Cambre Abbey, this is a prime example of the neo-Gothic style. Inside it's amazingly light, with pseudo-Gothic confessionals, and at the entrance on the right-hand side there's a

display of faded postcards that will delight every collector.

❺ Cocoon★★★

41, rue de la Paix
☎ 02 512 64 86
Mon.-Sat. 10.30am-6pm.

Why not get ahead of fashion? Dominique has an exclusive range of clothes for men and women, consisting of a few

designs from the next year's collections of some of fashion's top names. The result is knock-down prices, with a limited choice in any size, but a constant flow of new stock. A great place to find clothes that stand out from the crowd (extra-large sizes available) with fun accessories and helpful advice from the owner.

❻ Campion★★

15, rue Saint-Boniface
☎ 02 512 17 21
Mon.-Sat. 10am-1pm
and 2-6.30pm.

A haunt of professional photographers and demanding connoisseurs. The shop has a collection of cameras dating back to the early 20th century. Some of these antiques are for sale, as is a range of excellent secondhand equipment.

❼ Touijar★★

7, rue du Prince-Royal
☎ 02 511 41 78
Tue.-Sat. 10am-6.30pm.

Original pieces of jewelry created by using a combination of techniques and metals. Contemporary pieces show their multicultural origins: heavy gold necklaces, broad bracelets engraved with hieroglyphs, stones in natural settings. Every piece is unique and would embellish even a top designer outfit.

❽ YAMATO★★

A little bit of Tokyo, where Japanese men in suits and ties meet fans of *gyoza* and *sake* over a bowl of soup. Sixteen seats at the bar and a bench where you can kill time trying to understand the cartoons written in ideograms. Don't try lingering over your empty bowl or coming in a large party.

11, rue Francart – ☎ 02 502 28 93
Tue.-Fri. 12-2pm and 7-10pm, Sat. 12-2pm
and 6.30-9.30pm (closed Thu. lunchtime).

Around Grand-Place

Listed as one of Unesco's World Heritage Sites, Grand-Place (main square) is lined with old guild houses. Burned down during the shelling carried out on the orders of Louis XVI in 1695, it was rebuilt in four years, with even more baroque flourishes, in a mix of Flemish and Italian styles.

Hôtel de Ville

The building of the town hall started in 1402 and it remains the only evidence of the original Gothic architecture on Grand-Place. Particularly remarkable are its ornate façade and its spire topped by the archangel Michael killing the devil. This work of art by Martin van Rode, 5m (14ft) high and set on a pivot so it can be used as a weather vane, was hoisted up in 1455 when the building was completed.

Musée de la Ville de Bruxelles

The town museum was erected in the 16th century during the reign of Charles V. It was entirely rebuilt during the 19th century in a flamboyant neo-Gothic style. Here you can find

works of art, tapestries, retables as well as the entire impressive wardrobe of the Mannekenpis, no less than 654 suits!

Galeries royales Saint-Hubert

You can reach these galleries from the rue du Marché-aux-Herbes. In 1847 the galleries became the favorite place of the inhabitants of Brussels to stroll in and a fashionable rendez-vous for all types of intellectuals. Divided into three

sections, the 'Galerie du Roi', the 'Galerie de la Reine' and the 'Galerie des Princes', they house elegant shops today.

PRACTICAL INFORMATION

Grand-Place
(see pp. 38-41)
Metro Gare Centrale
☎ 02 279 43 55
Tue.-Sun. 10am-5pm.
Closed Jan. 1, May 1,
Nov. 1 & 11, Dec. 25.
Entrance charge.

Musée des
Instruments de musique

Housed since June 2000 in the magnificent former Old England stores, the Musical Instruments Museum (MIM) has nearly 7,000 items on display. It is one of the finest and richest collections of musical instruments in the world. A lifelike setting full of surprises will help you discover an often neglected universe.

The history

In 1898 the Old England company asked the Belgian architect, Paul Saintenoy, to build a prestigious iron and glass extension to the neo-classical building of Barnabé Guimard. This district, however, became gradually run down during the 1960s and the company moved to another location. It was only after extensive renovations that the MIM had the privilege of being housed in these impressive buildings.

The Snoeck and Contarini-Correr collections

The collection of César Snoek (a solicitor from Resnais) offers an extensive overview of instrument making in Belgium. The collection of Contarini-Correr (an important Venetian family) is made up of Italian and German instruments from the 16th and 17th centuries: violas da gamba, harpsichords, organs, and so on – a fascinating universe.

An impressive collection

Today, the MIM collection includes scraped or plucked string instruments, wind, percussion and electronic instruments from all over the world and from all periods, from pre-history to the present day. Don't forget to inquire about weekend concerts (3pm).

PRACTICAL INFORMATION

(see p. 49)
2, rue Montagne-de-la-Cour; trams 92-93-94 (Royale stop)
☎ 02 545 01 30
www.mim.fgov.be
Tue.-Fri. 9.30am-5pm, Sat.-Sun. 10am-5pm. Closed Jan. 1, May 1, Nov. 1 & 11, Dec. 25. Entrance charge (except on the first Wed. of the month from 1pm).

Musées royaux
des Beaux-Arts

These two museums, linked by an interior staircase, comprise the largest museum complex in Belgium. Their rich collections give an overview of the arts from the 14th century to the present day.

expressionism – including Permeke – you'll see creations by less well-known Belgian artists who deserve to be rediscovered. A section devoted to contemporary trends is periodically updated according to new acquisitions.

Musée d'Art ancien

Founded by Napoleon in 1801, this museum of ancient art displays wonderful paintings and sculptures from the end of the 14th to the 19th century. The Northern schools are particularly well represented, with major works by Bruegel the Elder, Rubens, Van der Weyden, Memling, Bosch, Jordaens and Van Dyck. Germany, Italy and France also have a significant presence.

Musée d'Art moderne

Opened in 1984, the Museum of Modern Art displays, over eight levels, artworks from the 19th and 20th centuries including works by Ingres and some conceptual art. Don't miss the rooms devoted to Delvaux, Magritte, Rik Wouters, Spilliaert and Marcel Broodhaerts. As well as the famous names from the Cobra group and from Flemish

PRACTICAL INFORMATION

(see p. 49)
3, rue de la Régence
☎ 02 508 32 11
www.fine-arts-museum.be
Tue.-Sun. 10am-5pm.
Closed Jan. 1, May 1, Nov. 1 & 11, Dec. 25.
Entrance charge (except on the first Wed. of the month from 1pm).

Around the Place Royale

The current site of Place Royale was occupied by the houses of the Dukes of Brabant (from the 11th century onwards), and the Dukes of Burgundy (15th and 16th centuries). In 1731, a fire completely destroyed the area. Charles of Lorraine, who was governor of the town at the end of the 18th century, took it upon himself to create a 'Royal Square' from scratch, surrounded by new buildings.

Aula Magna

Excavations under Place Royale uncovered the remains of the old ceremonial room used by the Dukes of Burgundy – the Aula Magna, built during the reign of Philip the Good – and of the imperial chapel where Charles V is said to have abdicated in 1555 in favor of his son, Philip II.

Palais Royal

The building of this royal palace started at the same time as that of Place Royale, and was completed in 1909. Here you can visit (from July 22 to September 5) magnificent ceremonial rooms such as the throne room and the mirror hall. At the far end of the right-hand gallery, don't miss the Hotel Bellevue which now houses a museum illustrating the history of the monarchy in Belgium. You'll discover the urbanization plans of Leopold II and the ethnographic journeys of Leopold III. A journey of discovery through rooms covering nearly 1000m^2 (10,750ft^2).

Parc Royal

This royal park was also designed at the end of the 18th century, in a very classical French style. Today, its wide avenues edged by trees, its fountains and its statues invite you on a walk in another era.

PRACTICAL INFORMATION

(see pp. 48-49)
Musée Bellevue and the Coudenberg archeological site
7, place des Palais (Metro Trône) ☎ 02 545 08 00
www.musbellevue.be
Jun.-Sep.: Tue.-Sun. 10am-6pm; Oct.-May: Tue.-Sun. 10am-5pm. Closed Jan. 1, Easter Sunday, May 1, Dec. 25. Entrance charge (free guided tours Tue. 3pm and Thu. 10.30am/3pm).
Palais Royal
☎ 02 551 34 00
www.monarchie.be
Tours 22 Jul.-5 Sep. Tue.-Sun. 10.30am-4.30pm. Entrance free.

Parc du Cinquantenaire

This park is one of the great urbanization projects launched by Leopold II. Created in 1880 to host the jubilee celebrations commemorating 50 years of the kingdom, the palace is centered around an arch topped by a *quadriga* (four-horse chariot sculpture) and decorated by statues of women symbolizing the nine Belgian provinces. From that same period, the Bordiau hall, with its impressive architecture of iron and glass, today houses two museums.

Autoworld

Before the Second World War, the automobile industry was one of the flagships of Belgian manufacturing, with makes like Minerva, Imperia, Germain and Vivinus. Under the vast glass dome of the Bordiau hall are gathered 400 vehicles, all in working order. It is one of the most renowned collections in Europe. You'll be able to rediscover the history of the 2CV, the Beetle, the Czechoslovakian Tatra, as well as seeing some rare models that once belonged to celebrities like J.F. Kennedy.

Musée royal de l'Armée et d'Histoire militaire

Inaugurated in 1923, this military museum houses, among other things, old weapons and armor. The 'air' section is probably the most surprising, with its 80 flying machines on display: a suspended Caravelle seems to fly through the air, and on the ground a DC3, bombers and various types of fighter planes seem about to take off!

PRACTICAL INFORMATION

Autoworld
(see p. 62)
11, parc du Cinquantenaire
Metro Mérode
☎ 02 736 41 65
www.autoworld.be
Every day 10am-6pm (5pm Oct.-Apr.), closed Dec. 25 and Jan. 1. Entrance charge.
Musée royal de l'Armée et d'Histoire militaire
3, parc du Cinquantenaire.
☎ 02 737 78 11
www.klm-mra.be
Every day except Mon. 9am-noon and 1-4.30pm, closed Jan. 1 May 1, Nov. 1 and Dec. 25. Entrance free.

Musées royaux
d'Art et d'Histoire

Non-European civilizations

Although the archeological and ethnographical collections from pre-Columbian America and Polynesia are exceptional – notice in particular the feather coat, called 'Moctezuma,' and the statue from Easter Island – try not to miss the artworks from China, Cambodia and India during your visit.

The royal art and history collections, or 'musée du Cinquantenaire,' are also housed in the stone, glass and metal building of the Belgian architect Bordiau. This complex is part of a truly universalist and encyclopedic project. There are four main sections: Antiquity, National Archeology – from prehistory to the Merovingians – European decorative arts from the Middle Ages to today, and non-European civilizations.

Antiquity

The Middle East, Egypt, Greece and Rome; in this section make sure you see the mosaics uncovered during the excavations in Apamee in Syria, the largest of which – representing hunting scenes – used to adorn the floor of a house in the 5th century AD.

The decorative arts

In addition to magnificent retables from the Brabant region (15th and 16th century), this section includes the Treasure Room where splendid items from the Middle Ages – shrines, altars, triptychs – are displayed, as well as a world famous collection of Mosan art.

PRACTICAL INFORMATION

(see p. 62) 10, parc du Cinquantenaire
Metro Mérode
☎ 02 741 72 11
www.kmkg-mrah.be
Tue.-Fri. 9.30am-5pm, Sat.-Sun. 10am-5pm. Closed Jan. 1, May 1, Nov. 1 & 11, Dec. 25. Entrance charge (except first Wed. of the month from 1pm).

Maison Cauchie

Thanks to its owners, Guy and Léo De Cissy, you can now visit the house that the architect, painter and decorator Paul Cauchie had built for himself in 1905. Ten years of restoration were necessary to preserve this art-nouveau gem in which you can see both the influence of the Glasgow school and the rigor of the Mackintosh style.

The house

In this house-cum-workshop, Cauchie displayed his art and displayed his preference for the geometry of shapes over the abstract, fluid and plant-like curves of Victor Horta. He rehabilitated the prestige of pictorial decor and interior design.

Sgraffiti

The sgraffiti created for this house are incredibly beautiful. On the façade, all the sgraffiti, with the exception of the motto "Par Nous Pour Nous" (by us,

for us) by Paul and Lisa Cauchie, were carefully taken down, then put back into place after the restoration of the house. This was a first in Belgium. These murals, inspired by pre-Raphaelite drawings and representing stylized muses, embellished the surround of a curved window.

The interior

When the house was restored, magnificent sgraffiti were discovered under the wallpaper in the dining room. They only needed to be cleaned to reveal

the original colors. Some items of furniture were found in the cellar and some ancient documents enabled the whole house to be restored to its original glory. If you are visiting in a small group, you may be lucky enough to see the bedroom and bathroom on the second floor.

PRACTICAL INFORMATION

(see p. 63)
5, rue des Francs
☎ 02 673 15 06
or 02 733 86 84
Open first weekend of each month, 11am-1pm/2-6pm. Entrance charge.

Centre belge de la
Bande Dessinée

This fascinating visit will enable you to improve your knowledge of comic-strip art and to have fun by following the history of comics. The museum has been set up with admirable simplicity in the former Vaucquez stores, built in 1906 by the ubiquitous Victor Horta.

The building

Initially the building was only meant to house wholesale cloth traders, but the architect took care over every detail to integrate the industrial requirements with the aesthetics. A huge staircase adorned with extraordinary bannisters leads to the two floors lit by a vast rooflight. Don't forget to look at the façade. Today, this building, rescued by the project to set up a center for comics, is the only survivor out of the six department stores designed by Victor Horta.

The history

Did you know that comics appeared at about the same time as art nouveau? They were born in Belgium in 1929 with *Tintin* in *Le Petit Vingtième*. For his character, Hergé drew his inspiration from *Zig et Puce* by Alain Saint-Ogan in France. Then came the era of *Bob et Bobette*, of the weekly *Spirou* and the famous *Journal de Tintin*.

The birth of a comic

You'll be able to view some 300 original plates out of a collection of around 5,000 that are regularly displayed. You'll follow the different stages in the creation of a comic, from sketching to printing; another room is dedicated to the most famous characters in this field. You'll not have time to get bored!

PRACTICAL INFORMATION

(see p. 13)
20, rue des Sables
Bus 38 (Berlaimont)
www.comicscenter.net
☎ 02 219 19 80
Tue.-Sun. 10am-6pm,
closed Jan. 1 and Dec. 25. Entrance charge.

Musée royal
de l'Afrique centrale

In existence since the independence of the Congo, the Museum of Central Africa is one part of a vast scientific institute that takes an interest in other African nations, as well as in the Americas and Oceania. An unusual visit which is worth the trip from Brussels.

The origins of the museum

Built between 1904 and 1910 by the French architect Charles Girault at the request of Leopold II, this building first housed a world research center for Africa, Asia and the Far East, authorized to train specialists to work in the colonies.

Nature and culture

Zoology rooms display animals from the African continent, sometimes in a recreated natural habitat. You'll find out all there is to know about the elephant or the tsetse fly. In the geology rooms, you'll be able to admire numerous stones and minerals. But the 'must see' in the museum is without doubt its wonderful ethnographic collection: African masks, sculptures, everyday and ornamental objects, musical instruments. You'll be carried away to another continent.

History

Other sections retrace the prehistory of the African continent through archeological items and glass cabinets devoted to paleontology. You'll also be able to revisit the history of the exploration of Central Africa, and the Belgian presence in the Congo.

PRACTICAL INFORMATION

13, Leuvensesteenweg, Tervueren 3080
From Brussels, at Montgomery metro, take tram 44 to the terminus (45 minutes).
☎ 02 769 52 11
www.africamuseum.be
Tue.-Fri. 10am-5pm, Sat.-Sun. 10am-6pm, closed Mondays and Jan. 1, May 1, Dec. 25. Entrance charge.

Musée David et
Alice van Buuren

This house-cum-museum is little known yet it is a real treasure of art-deco interior design and architecture. David van Buuren, initially a financier, soon became a collector and a patron of the arts. With his wife, Alice, he commissioned many artists, architects and decorators to build their house in 1928. It was fitted out with remarkable homogeneity by Belgian, French and Dutch interior designers.

The house

The staircase, made entirely of rosewood and embellished with stained-glass windows, was made by the 'Dominique' studio in Paris. In the dining room, marvellous carpets by Maurice Dufrêne enhance the soft color of the sycamore furniture created by the firm J. Wynants from Malines. A pure style where the line and the refined exotic materials highlight the beautiful collection of old paintings.

The garden

This large 1.5ha (3.75 acre) garden is divided into three parts: the Picturesque Garden, wild and lush, planted by Jules Buyssens in 1924 in the spirit of the Roaring Twenties; the Secret Garden of the Heart created in 1970 by the landscape architect René Péchère as a homage to Alice van Buuren, and the Maze.

The maze

The paths, edged with yews, follow the gentle slope of the grounds leading to the large cedar tree, the lair of the Minotaur. If you don't go wrong, you'll follow a 380m (1,250ft) trail, along which you'll meet seven statues illustrating the *Song of Songs*. If you are unfortunate enough to get lost, you'll need to cover a few hundred extra meters!

PRACTICAL INFORMATION

41, avenue Léo Errera
Trams 23-90 (Churchill stop), bus 60
(see p. 23)
☎ 02 343 48 51
www.museumvan
buuren.com
Open every day except
Tue. 2-5.30pm.
Entrance charge.

Practicalities

Hotels

Modern hotels are centered around the European institutions, whereas the old palaces are situated along the Adolphe-Max boulevard. Near Grand-Place you'll find only one splendid classy hotel, the Dixseptième, the others being small modest establishments that are still preferable to hotel chains. Finally, if you have a car, charming hotels in an idyllic setting can be found only 10 or 20 minutes' drive from the town center.

Ratings

Hotels can be divided into four categories: former palaces from the Belle Epoque (Edwardian period) that have been renovated, hotels belonging to international chains, new charming 4- or 5-star hotels where care is taken to provide a refined decor, and finally a few small independent 2- and 3-star hotels, often large impressive former houses that have been adapted, where you'll find a friendly family welcome and various degrees of comfort. So that you can enjoy your weekend, we have decided to mention only hotels that stand out, either because of their decor and the warmth of their welcome, or because they have affordable prices all the year round. Although luxury hotels slash their prices (more than 50% discount) at weekends, a double bedroom (breakfast included) will still cost you €100 to €150. Allow €75–€95 for a 3-star hotel whereas 2-star hotels vary between €50 and €90 for a double bedroom. If the hotel has a garage, there is often a charge, but breakfast (which is usually plentiful) is included, except for large hotels during the week. Low-season prices apply in 4- and 5- star hotels during the Christmas holiday and in July and August.

Reservations

To reserve, all you need do is give your details and your credit card number by phone, fax or email. Bank transfers or eurocheques are also accepted for deposits. The cost of one night will be charged if you do not honor the booking. Reserve well in advance to increase your chance of getting a good room at a weekend rate. Moreover, it is advisable to specify the type of

FINDING YOUR WAY

Next to each address in the Where to stay, Shopping and Going Out sections, we have given details of the nearest Brussels metro, tram or bus station.

room you wish to have. Most hotels are affiliated members of **Bruxelles International Tourisme** :

☎ 02 513 74 84

✆ 02 513 83 20

tourism@brusselsinter national.be

This is a free booking service run by the tourist office where you're likely to be able to deal with an English-speaking person.

Last-minute reservations

If you are in Brussels and are looking for a room for that night or the following night, head for the Bruxelles-Tourisme (tourist office) on Grand-Place.

Bed and Breakfast

Bed and breakfast is a convivial formula and offers a different approach to discovering the city. Whether a single room with shared bathroom, en suite bedroom or a room in a prestigious setting, prices vary accordingly from €55 to €100 for two people. For a list of bed and breakfasts, contact:

Bed & Brussels,

9, rue Kindermans

☎ 02 646 07 37

✆ 02 644 01 14

www.bnb-brussels.be

Renting an apartment

For one day, one weekend or one week, renting a flat with all the services of a hotel is a clever formula that is not necessarily more costly than staying in a hotel. This is what

the Mas Residence offers. Tastefully decorated, these flats cost between €170 and €210 for one weekend for areas varying between 30m^2 and 64m^2 (320ft^2 and 680ft^2).

Mas Residence :

18, rue de Spa

☎ 02 230 59 50

✆ 02 230 26 50

www.masapartments.com

Restaurants

Judging by the number of people at the tables, there is no doubt that food continues to be one of the major interests of the Belgians. The idea that Belgian gastronomy is limited to mussels and fries is far from the truth. French cuisine is the most appreciated, but there are also some interesting discoveries to be made in the local cuisine, such as prawn croquettes, dishes stewed in beer, and fish specialties from the North Sea. In a

cosmopolitan town like Brussels, you can also treat your tastebuds to world cuisine. Choosing is not always easy, so remember these three rules above all: an empty restaurant by 8pm is not a good sign, a very trendy decor is rarely synonymous with good food, still-life paintings displayed in front of restaurants in the vicinity of Grand-Place should alert you to tourist traps. If you don't know where to go, head for the pretty Place du Châtelain where you'll find many fashionable restaurants

What price?

Restaurants are fairly expensive. Allow a minimum of €30 per person for an average restaurant; the bill will rise rapidly if you go to a gastronomic restaurant. But it is always possible to eat out on a small budget in one of the many *table d'hôtes* which abound in the town or in snack bars where you'll find simple affordable food. Prices include a 15 percent service charge, but it is customary to leave a small tip, especially in the more prestigious restaurants. Valet parking, very fashionable, also comes at a cost. Apart from a few exceptions, you can usually settle your bill with a credit card.

BRUSSELS TIME

Food is usually served quite late, up until 11pm or even midnight. Some restaurants, such as the Falstaff, are open 24 hours a day, but this tends to be the exception. Most restaurants close on Saturday lunchtimes and on Sundays, but you can still find some good ones open on those days. Finally, brunch is becoming increasingly popular, with a trend toward a full buffet at affordable prices.

Hotels

1 - Monty
2 - Amigo
3 - Beverly-Hills
4 - Monty

Îlot Sacré

Amigo★★★★★

1-3, rue de l'Amigo
Metro Bourse
☎ 02 547 47 47
📠 02 502 28 05
www.roccofortehotels.com

A stone's throw from Grand-Place, this neo-Renaissance building houses one of the pleasantest hotels in the capital city. The prices of the 174 luxurious rooms, decorated with much attention to detail in monochrome shades of blue, red or green, vary according to the size and the view over the Hôtel de Ville (from €229 at weekends).

To spend an memorable night, the Blaton suite, an apartment with a superb terrace on the top floor, is a €1,500 extravagance, champagne and dinner by candlelight included. There's a fitness center, a garage (extra charge) and a minimalist atmosphere in Bocconi, the hotel's classy Italian restaurant, using seasonal produce.

Le Dixseptième★★★★

25, rue de la Madeleine
Metro Gare Centrale
☎ 02 502 57 44
📠 02 502 64 24
www.ledixseptieme.be

The monumental Louis-XVI staircase and salons decorated with frescoes have been preserved in this lovely gabled house, formerly the residence of the Spanish ambasssador in the early 18th century. Every room has its own character: from the very large rooms with fireplaces, parquet flooring and mottled furnishings, to attic rooms with exposed beams and rustic furniture, to the more modern studios looking out over a leafy patio. Refined, quality service, with an excellent breakfast.

La Madeleine★★

22, rue de la Montagne
Metro Gare Centrale
☎ 02 513 29 73
📠 02 502 13 50
www.hotel-la-madeleine.be

This 17th-century residence suffered a rather extreme form of renovation, which preserved nothing but the façade, behind which you'll find 52 comfortable though small rooms (apart from the larger, executive suites). It does, however, have the advantage of being one of the good affordable hotels close to Grand-Place.

Hôtel Saint-Michel★★

15, Grand-Place
Metro Bourse or Gare Centrale
☎ 02 511 09 56
✆ 02 511 46 00
www.hotelsaintmichel.be

This is a very small hotel in the prestigious structure of the house of the Dukes of Brabant, where seven rooms have windows onto Grand-Place. A box overlooking 'the richest theater in the world' is fairly expensive for a hotel of this category, but the show (particularly the Ommegang in July) is worth the extra. There's an elevator and you can have breakfast in your room.

Quartier Sainte-Catherine

Welcome★★★

23, quai au Bois-à-Brûler
Metro Sainte-Catherine
☎ 02 219 95 46
✆ 02 217 18 87
www.brusselswelcomehotel.com

In the little preserved area of the former Béguinage, this small hotel, with 17 rooms, is big on comfort and flowery decor. Exemplary welcome and service, peace and quiet guaranteed and free parking. It's excellent value and in an interesting quarter with the best fish restaurants in town.

Hôtel Atlas★★★

30, rue du Vieux-Marché-aux-Grains
Metro Bourse or Ste-Catherine
☎ 02 502 60 06
✆ 02 502 69 35
www.atlas.be

The lovely stone façade hides 88 well-appointed rooms that are surprisingly quiet for this trendy area, with a view over either the courtyard or the shady square. The decor is sober in basic colors and the family welcoming. A double surprise awaits you in the breakfast room: a generous and varied buffet and part of the 11th-century city wall. Excellent value for money.

Résidence Les Écrins★★

15, rue du Rouleau
Metro Sainte-Catherine
☎ 02 219 36 57
✆ 02 223 57 40
www.lesecrins.com

Within the Béguinage, this century-old private house has been converted into a pleasant 11-room home where you are warmly welcomed. The spacious modern rooms, with functional furniture and TV, are equipped with fine bathrooms, except for two less expensive rooms whose bathroom is on the landing. The reasonable prices for the district (€60 to €85) include a copious breakfast with croissants, orange juice and eggs.

De Brouckère

Métropole★★★★★

31, place De Brouckère
Metro De Brouckère
☎ 02 217 23 00
✆ 02 218 02 20
www.metropolehotel.be

This is the finest of all the Belle Époque grand hotels, with a profusion of Numidian marble, gilded bronze and columns, has just celebrated its centenary. Sample both the acclaimed cuisine of Dominique Michou accompanied by the wine you have brought with you (Wednesdays only), and the thalasso-therapy center. On the other hand, the rooms vary greatly in quality, the ones at the front being the brightest. You're most likely to get a good room at the weekend rate in summer.

Le Plaza★★★★★

118-126, boulevard Adolphe-Max
Metro Rogier
☎ 02 278 01 00
✆ 02 278 01 01
www.leplaza-brussels.be

A grand hotel dating from 1930 designed by Michel Polak. Admirably restored in 1996, it has 193 rooms, including some suites, in which the discreet luxury of the delicate fabrics and period woodwork combine harmoniously with the modern bathrooms. Apart from Winston Churchill, the most notable guests have generally been great names from the music hall and French cinema – including Simone Signoret and Louis Jouvet. The restaurant has a trompe l'œil dome, and other attractions include an old movie theater, amethyst crystal chandeliers and an authentic Gobelin tapestry. Garage parking is available for a charge.

Crowne Plaza City Centre★★★★

3, rue Gineste
Metro Rogier
☎ 02 203 62 00
✆ 02 203 40 11
www.crowneplazabrussels.com

Built in 1910 in a very modernist style by A. Pompe, this hotel has witnessed the varying fortunes of the 20th century: art deco, World War II, a new look for Expo' 58, renovation in 1982 after a narrow escape from property developers and an American franchise in 2000. The period furniture, found in the cellars, has been put back into the rooms, giving them an added touch of originality. Ask for room 651, a jewel of art nouveau, or a room overlooking the park. If you have the means, you can always request the suite where Grace Kelly stayed in 1956.

Le Coudenberg

Astoria ★★★★★

103, rue Royale
Metro Botanique
☎ 02 227 05 05
📠 02 217 11 50
www.sofitel.be

A monumental entrance lined with granite columns, a gilded neo-Victorian hall lit by thousands of lights, a majestic staircase and a restaurant with an excellent reputation. This Belle-Epoque palace 'by appointment to His Majesty the King', where some royal receptions still take place, accommodated the young Emperor Hirohito in 1921. You can have a drink in its Orient Express-style bar, listen to one of the Sunday concerts, stay in the most luxurious of suites or in a room that's less expensive but just as comfortable. Best are rooms 117, 126, 127 and 129.

Hôtel du Congrès ★★★

42, rue du Congrès
Metro Madou
☎ 02 217 18 90
📠 02 217 18 97
www.hotelducongres.be

This hotel in a quiet area has the comfortable atmosphere of two

private houses whose 77 rooms, may lack character, but all have a shower, WC and television. To get your day off to a good start, breakfast includes Viennese pastries, cereals, fruit and Belgian specialty breads. The parking lot has seven places, you'll get a good welcome and there's a promotional rate at weekends. Reserve in advance.

Sabina ★★

78, rue du Nord
Metro Madou
☎ 02 218 26 37
📠 02 219 32 39
www.hotelsabina.com

A 19th-century bourgeois house with wood paneling and moldings, offering 24 light, quiet, well-equipped rooms, all with television. Modest prices and a friendly welcome.

Ixelles and Saint-Gilles

Manos premier ★★★★★

100-106, chaussée de Charleroi
Trams 91-92 (Faider)
☎ 02 537 96 82
📠 02 539 36 55
www.manoshotel.com

In the heart of the art-nouveau district, a lovely old-style hotel full of oriental carpets, crystal chandeliers, gilding and marble. Its major advantage, apart from the pleasant rooms, is an enormous garden where chickens lay the eggs for breakfast, which is served outside on fine days. An oasis of pleasure at €115 for the weekend.

Rembrandt ★★

42, rue de la Concorde
Metro Louise or trams 93-94 (Stéphanie)
☎ 02 512 71 39
📠 02 511 71 36
www.hotel-rembrandt.be

A stone's throw from the smart stores on Avenue Louise, this building is on the corner of a quiet street and has 13 light-filled rooms. Very well kept, with a lovely smell of wax, this is an ideal family hotel for those who set store by the welcome they receive. Depending on your budget, you can either have a suite in the attic (no. 15), the very pleasant no. 6 with its little lounge, or one of the more modest rooms.

Beverly-Hills ★★★

71, rue du Prince-Royal
Metro Louise or trams 93-94 (Stéphanie)
☎ 02 513 22 22
📠 02 513 87 77
www.hotelbeverlyhills.be

This hotel was built in 2001 and is ideally located in a quiet street near avenue Louise and the luxury stores. Among the 30 cozy rooms, all equipped with modern comforts, you might prefer the four attic rooms with exposed beams. You'll find a warm welcome and bargain prices at weekends (€84 breakfast included).

Cinquantenaire

Stanhope ★★★★★

9, rue du Commerce
Metro Trône
☎ 02 506 91 11
📠 02 512 17 08
www.stanhope.be

This hotel in the 'European' area is a high spot of English-style refinement with 50 light very comfortable rooms. The penthouse at the end of the garden is ideal for a romantic (if pricey) weekend. You will find personalized service, garage parking for an extra charge and an excellent restaurant, which sadly is closed on Saturdays and Sundays.

1 - Amigo
2 - Amigo
3 - Monty

Montgoméry★★★★★

134, av. de Tervueren
Metro Montgoméry
☎ 02 741 85 11
📠 02 741 85 00
www.montgomery.be

The new façade conceals all the comfort of an old English stately home. The spacious rooms come with a choice of three atmospheres: rural, British with a flowery dash of Vichy France, or colonial. Lovely and cozy, there's a library with a log fire, interesting books and deep sofas, where generous breakfasts are served at weekends. Other attractions include a garage and weekend rates (the third night from Saturday to Sunday is free).

Monty★★

101, boulevard Brand
Whitlock
Metro Georges-Henri
☎ 02 734 56 36
📠 734 50 05
www.monty-hotel.be

In this middle-class district you encounter the surprise of an affluent-looking house transformed into a designer hotel. The 18 standard rooms equipped with state-of-the-art bathrooms are decorated in grey and red. If you want quiet, you'll prefer the rooms overlooking the yard. The copious breakfast is included in the price, which is slightly high for this category (from €85 to €130).

In surrounding areas

Les Tourelles★★★

135, avenue Winston-Churchill
Bus 60 or trams 23-90 (Cavell)
☎ 02 344 95 73
📠 02 346 42 70
www.lestourelles.be

Not far from La Cambre Wood, in a very peaceful district, this delightful manor house with a magnolia tree outside was, until 1934, a boarding school for young ladies from good families. It has retained this rather outdated character in its lounges and in 20 rooms, all of which are equipped with a bathroom. Ask for a room on the first floor with a balcony overlooking the courtyard. It's better to reserve in advance, particularly when there's a tournament at the neighboring Léo Tennis Club.

Le Manoir du Lac★★★★

4, avenue Hoover
☎ 655 63 11
📠 655 64 55.

Twenty minutes by car from Brussels and five minutes from Genval train station, a flower-bedecked cottage nestling in a garden full of rare plants. Very romantic with its English-style lounge and terrace, where you can breakfast in the sun. It also has a sauna and a Turkish bath for real relaxation. Lots to see and do in the local area (Lake Genval) either on foot or by bicycle. Very good prices at weekends (€130 for a double).

Restaurants

1 - Aux Bons Enfants
2 - Tan
3 - L'Étoile d'Or
4 - Belga Queen

dishes such as salmon mille feuilles, lobster and crayfish tails and grilled calf's sweetbreads. It's a bit expensive, but worth the price.

Îlot Sacré

Aux Armes de Bruxelles★★★

13, rue des Bouchers
Metro Bourse
☎ 02 511 55 50
Tue.-Sun. noon-11pm
Closed from mid-June to mid-July.

A Brussels institution serving authentic local cuisine, mainly poultry and North Sea fish, as well as beef *carbonade* with gueuze beer or Brussels *potée*, or boiled meat with cabbage. Make sure you sample the lobster *waterzoi* and Zeeland mussels.

A specialty meal washed down with muscadet costs €44.50.

De l'Ogenblik★★★

1, galerie des Princes
Metro Bourse
☎ 02 511 61 51
Lunchtime and evening
Closed Sun. and lunchtime on public holidays.

This restaurant in a corner of Galerie Saint-Hubert is one of the most highly rated in the area and is frequented by artists. Delicious French cuisine with a menu that changes every day according to available ingredients, as well as a few reliable

La Taverne du Passage★★★

30, galerie de la Reine
Metro Gare Centrale
☎ 02 512 37 31
Every day noon-midnight
Closed Wed.-Thu. in June and July.

No one can claim to know Brussels until they've visited this venerable art-deco brasserie and sampled the sublime shrimp croquettes. Some good wine and delicious Belgian and French specialties, but sadly the service has gone downhill in recent times.

Saint-Géry

In't Spinnekopje★★

1, place du Jardin-aux-Fleurs
Metro Bourse
☎ 02 511 86 95
Mon.-Fri. lunchtime and evening. Closed Sat. lunchtime and Sun.

The stagecoach no longer stops out-side this 1762 inn, but inside they still speak *Brusseleir* and serve dependably good local dishes. If you like beer, so much the better, as there's plenty around in both the drinking glasses and cooking pots, from the *carbo-nades* with lambic to the filet steak with gueuze beer and guinea fowl with raspberry beer. It's also one of the few places where you can drink *faro*.

La Manufacture

12-20, rue Notre-Dame-du-Sommeil
Tram 18 (Porte de Ninove)
☎ 02 502 25 25
Lunchtime and evening
Closed Sat. lunchtime and Sun.

A pleasure for the eyes and taste buds in the industrial setting of the former Delvaux tannery workshops. The owners have played on the mix of materials (steel, concrete and leather) and of cuisines (French, Belgian and Oriental). The result is a tempura of Belgian cheeses with date and apple syrup (€12.30), followed by a grilled red tuna steak, with a white truffle dressing (€18.80) or Peking duck with honey (€17.40). Wines from all over the world, huge and pleasant terrace and valet parking for the rather well-groomed clients.

Quartier Sainte-Catherine

Vismet★★★

23, place Sainte-Catherine
Metro Sainte-Catherine

☎ 02 218 85 45
Lunchtime and evening
Closed Sun. and Mon.

A kind of modern brasserie provides an simple setting for the high-flying cuisine prepared with flair by Tom Decroos, trained in some of the country's classiest restaurants. A triumphant blend of intuitive recipes and fresh produce supplied by his father, an Ostend fisherman. As well as Belgian classics, like shrimp croquettes and poached cod in muslin sauce, the menu is changed every month to incorporate several tasty surprises. (The swordfish in citrus fruit and pepper served with candied vegetables is a delight!) Cost is about €50, but you can get lunch during the week for €15.

La Belle Maraîchère★★★

11a, place Sainte-Catherine
Metro Sainte-Catherine

☎ 02 512 97 59
Lunchtime and evening except Wed. and Thu.

The best fish restaurant in the area (see p. 44-45).

De Brouckère

Roma★★★★

12-14, rue des Princes
Metro La Monnaie
☎ 02 219 01 94
Lunchtime and evening (until 1am on performance nights)
Closed Sat. lunchtime, Sun., Mon. and public holidays.

A classy interior next to the Théâtre de la Monnaie, with Italian cuisine to match. Besides the à la carte menu and set meal at €30 to €60 (wine included), there are dishes of the day according to availability, with an excellent choice of tastily prepared fish. Among the pasta specialties, try the sublime *agnolotti* (ravioli with cheese). All in all, excellent gourmet Italian cuisine accompanied by good Italian wines.

Belga Queen★★★★

32, rue Fossé-aux-Loups
Metro De Brouckère
☎ 02 217 21 87
Every day lunchtime and evening.

The latest venue of Antoine Pinto, award-winning chef and creator of sumptuous decors. In an

immense Empire hall covered with a glass roof, you dine on modern, low-fat Belgian cuisine. To go with your salmon in Rodenbach sauce, you have a choice of wines produced by Belgian winegrowers in France, Italy, Portugal and Spain. You might also like to visit the oyster bar, the bar-lounge and the cigar club located in the bank's former strong room, with live music from Thursday through Saturday. Note that there are two services in the evening up to midnight, and the bill can be steep (€75 à la carte).

Le Sablon

Trente rue de la paille★★★★

30, rue de la Paille
Bus 48 (Grand-Sablon)
☎ 02 512 07 15
Mon.-Fri. lunchtime and evening.

The varied menu specializes in tasty fish and meat. The dishes are imaginative and subtly flavored by the chef, André Martini. Set lunch consists of three courses for €31. Allow €60 to eat à la carte.

Aux Bons Enfants★★

49, place du Grand-Sablon
Bus 48 (Grand-Sablon)
☎ 02 512 40 95

Lunchtime and evening, except Tue. evening and Wed.

Here you are invited without undue fuss to sit down in front of a copious plate of homemade pasta, a tasty *osso bucco* or a grilled veal liver, washed down with good Italian wines. Franco, the owner of the place for 35 years, welcomes you warmly, as does this beautiful dwelling dating from 1567. As you can eat here very well for €20-25, it's always crowded so think about reserving and have cash ready. Credit cards are not accepted.

Les Marolles

L'Idiot du Village★★★★

19, rue Notre-Seigneur
Bus 48 (Chapelle)
☎ 02 502 55 82
Lunchtime and evening
Closed Sat.-Sun., Jul. 15 to Aug. 15 and Dec. 24-Jan 2.

A place where you can explore both beauty and flavor. Step through the velvet curtains into a dazz-ling, theatrical atmosphere and enjoy a very warm welcome. At a candlelit table you can sample delicious local dishes reinvented by the French chef, such as raw salmon *tartare* or scallops and foie gras. It's trendy, rather expensive, with a high class clientele (a favorite of King Albert and Queen Paola). Reservation recommended in the evening.

Les Larmes du Tigre★★★

21, rue De Wynants
Metro Louise
☎ 02 512 18 77
Lunchtime and evening
Closed Sat. lunch and Tue.

A real festival of Thai flavors in a subtle, exotic restaurant located behind the law courts. They serve a little sherbet between courses to aid digestion and the staff never stop smiling. Don't miss the buffet particularly on Sunday evenings when you have a wonderful choice at a very affordable price.

Ixelles and Saint-Gilles

Inada★★★★

73, rue de la Source
Metro Hôtel des Monnaies
☎ 02 538 01 13
Lunchtime and evening
Closed Sat. lunchtime-Mon. public holidays and mid-Dec. to mid-Jan.

1 - Tan
2 - L'Idiot du Village
3 - Vismet
4 - Toucan Brasserie

☎ 02 647 70 44
Every day 12-2.30pm and
7-11pm.

Healthy, tasty and good to look at. This is the creed of Emmanuel Verstraeten, who has turned this superb top-grade hotel into a place conceived along organic lines: the vitality of the color red, the tactile quality of the wood, the irreproachable

A very fine Japanese chef assisted by probably the best wine steward in Brussels serving French cuisine enhanced by subtle, Asiatic flavors. A real feast that you won't forget in a hurry

Tan★★★

95, rue de l'Aqueduc
☎ 02 537 87 87
Tram 81-82 (Trinité)
Tue.-Sat. lunchtime and evening.

This is an unusual restaurant that takes a new look at 'living foods.' For Pol Grégoire, the point of cooking is to eliminate toxins and bring out the 'life energy' of food. In his dishes there are lots of raw foodstuffs, aromatic plants, edible flowers and sprouting seeds, as well as fish and meat cooked on low heat. The result, rather surprisingly, is a potpourri of forgotten flavors. The wines and beers are, of course, organic, and smokers utterly banished. Although lunch costs €14.50 or

€17.50, to eat à la carte will come to around €40.

Rouge Tomate★★★

190, avenue Louise
Tram 93-94 (Lesbroussart)

FIVE-STAR EATING

Comme chez Soi★★★★★
23, place Rouppe
Metro Anneessens
☎ 02 512 29 21
Tue.-Sat. lunchtime and evening
Closed Jul., Christmas and New Year holidays.
You must make a reservation if you want to get a table in this temple of gastronomy and art-nouveau decor. At the helm is Pierre Wynants, who brings out the flavors of classic French cuisine with some Oriental influences. The vegetable mousse is truly a masterpiece. For those on a budget, there's a set menu at €64. Smart dress is recommended.

background music, and the dynamism of a Mediterranean cuisine based on olive oil and quality produce. The creativity of chef Fabrice Roche finds expression in straightforward cooking that coaxes the flavors from fish, vegetables and white meats seasoned with herbs. The clientele is rather fashionable, the garden welcoming in fine weather, and the check will come to around €40.

En face de Parachute★★★

578, chaussée de Waterloo
Bus 38 (Bascule)
☎ 02 346 47 41
Tue.-Fri. lunchtime and evening
Credit cards not accepted.
Reservation recommended in the evening.

This restaurant is packed with a trendy crowd who come to sample the dishes of the week created by Nounou. A great connoisseur of Bordeaux, if the wine list is anything to go by, but there are many other treasures in his well-stocked cellar. The cuisine is somewhere between French and Italian, with the chef's own inventive touch. A relaxed bistro atmosphere and lunchtime dish of the day for €13.20.

Around Place Brugmann

Toucan Brasserie

1, avenue Louis Lepoutre
Bus 60 (Tenbosch)
☎ 02 345 30 17
Every day lunchtime and evening, except Dec. 24, 25 and 31 and Jan 1.

A new-style brasserie, with a fashionably simple setting, serving classic menus tweaked to perfection by chef Jean-Pierre Gascoin. A gourmand's cuisine that will satisfy lovers of grilled chitterlings, tuna with tartar sauce, ginger and prunes, and

eggplant caviar. A special mention for the foie gras terrine and the crème brûlée with honey and saffron (delicious – really!), as well as the eclectic wine list. Service is caring and efficient, the price averaging around €30 each.

Le Cinquantenaire

Rosticceria Fiorentina★★

45, rue Archimède
Metro Schuman
☎ 02 734 92 36
Sun.-Mon. lunchtime and evening.

Good home cooking from chef Lucca in an unpretentious setting. Minestrone, pasta dishes roast veal with *faggioli* and *fegato*. In winter there's plenty of game. Dish of the day costs €15 served with Tuscan wine of course. A fine restaurant that hasn't yet been taken over by the Eurocrats who prefer a bit more luxury.

Saint-Boniface and place Flagey

Un peu beaucoup★★

22, rue de la Paix
Metro Porte de Namur
☎ 02 503 22 36
Lunchtime and evening, except Sat.-Sun. lunchtime

1 - Un peu beaucoup
2 - Belga Queen
3 - L'Idiot du Village
4 - Tan

2

The system is attractive. For €17.50, you can choose between an assortment of starters or desserts and a meat, fish or vegetarian main dish. The tasty and light cooking is based on world flavors combined with Belgian-French knowhow. Examples are poultry *tajine* with cardamom, lamb *chili con carne*, and *tiramisu* with *speculoos*. Good wines at affordable prices selected by a talented wine waiter, are served with this excellent homely cuisine.

Chez Marie★★★

40, rue Alphonse de Witte
Bus 71 and trams 81-82
(Flagey)
☎ 02 644 30 31
Lunchtime and evening
Closed Sat. lunchtime,
Sun.-Mon.

This smart café is hidden behind the church, decorated in warm shades, with heavy hangings, mirrors, candlesticks and leather seats. Lilian Devaux, a talented chef, and Daniel Marcil, one of the best wine waiters in the city

with a cellar of some 400 varieties, form a perfect pair. French cuisine with updated classical dishes such as cod *brandade* with crushed tomatoes and a purée of peppers, or fresh roasted cod-back with apple stuffed with lobster and mild curry. Set lunch costs €16.50, à la carte eating will cost €65-70.

ALSO

Easy Tempo p. 55
L'Écailler du Palais Royal p. 51-52
La Quincaillerie p. 56
L'Amadeus p. 59

Uccle

Le Pain et le Vin★★★

812a, chaussée
d'Alsemberg
Tram 55-Ritweger
☎ 02 332 37 74
Lunchtime and evening,
Closed Sat. lunchtime,
Sun.-Mon.

To eat and drink well is the creed of a talented chef and a wine waiter who have chosen a fine house decorated with taste in which to practice their art. The flavors are subtle, their inspiration French and Italian, their humor quite Belgian. And to accompany the very tasty cooking, a wine list of 200 types of wines that stray off the beaten track. Worth noting: a pleasant shady garden and lunch at €21.90.

Light meals
and tearooms

1 - Comocomo
2 - La Crèmerie de la Vache
3 - Passiflore
4 - Tapas Locas

Between visits or while on a shopping marathon, take time to have a break in one of these popular places, where you can enjoy bread and jam, soup or the dish of the day. In the afternoon some also serve pastries, but at tea time be sure to go to one of the best tearooms in the capital.

Fast food

Comocomo

19, rue Antoine Dansaert
Metro Bourse
☎ 02 503 03 30
Every day 12am-3pm and
7-11pm.

The idea here is to sit at the counter and choose dishes that move past you on a conveyor belt, according to your appetite and your preference. The specialty of the house is *pintxos* or tapas from the Basque country. It tastes good and is fun and affordable: €8.50 for three *pintxos* and and €14 for six. Note that on the first Tuesday of the month at 7pm there is a wine-tasting session of seven Spanish wines with seven *pintxos*. Appeals to trendy cosmopolitan customers.

Intermezzo

16, rue des Princes
Metro De Brouckère
☎ 02 218 03 11
Mon.-Sat. 12am-3pm,
Fri. 7-11pm.

A real Italian café in which to have a cup of coffee or a quick *bruschetta* or the pasta dish of the day (€8.50).

Osteria A l'Ombra

2, rue des Harengs
Metro Bourse or De Brouckère
☎ 02 511 67 10
Every day 12am-2.30pm and 6.30-11.30pm.
Closed Sat. lunchtime and Sun.

A Venetian-style *osteria* housed in an early 20th-century former fish-shop a stone's throw from Grand-Place, where you can still eat genuine *antipasti* and little Italian dishes washed down with a Prosecco or other excellent wines served by the glass.

Soepbar

89, rue Haute
Bus 48-20 (Chapelle)
☎ 02 511 10 18
Open 10am-6.30pm except Wed.

In the Marolles, a cosy atmosphere to eat simply. Choose one of the soups of the day – from the traditional tomato soup with *ballekes* (dumplings) to the gaspacho (from €4 to €5) – or a salad that comes in various versions, from the ultra-diet to more substantial ones (€9.50).

Comocomo

Le Pain quotidien

16, rue Antoine Dansaert
Metro Bourse
☎ 02 502 23 61
11, rue des Sablons
Bus 48 (Sablon)
☎ 02 513 51 54
124, avenue Louise
Trams 93-94 (Defacqz)
☎ 02 646 49 83
Mon.-Fri. 7.30am-7pm,
Sat.-Sun. 8am-7pm.

A large table of pale wood, fashionable varnished walls, a few pots of dried tomatoes and homemade preserves. The table d'hôte concept where you can eat tasty open sandwiches and mix with fashionable people, is becoming increasingly popular.

Tapas Locas

74, rue du Marché-au-Charbon
Metro Bourse

☎ 02 502 12 68
Wed.-Sun. 6pm-midnight
(1am Fri.-Sat.).

Enjoy a gargantuan meal of different *tapas* or savor a dish of octopus with *pimientos* (sweet peppers). Allow €3 a portion.

Tout Bon

68, rue du Luxembourg
Metro Trône
☎ 02 230 42 44
Every day 7am-8pm.

Opposite the Gare du Luxembourg, this is one of the best addresses for enjoying a copious breakfast with old-fashioned country bread, croissants, various jams, chocolate pasta and freshly-squeezed orange juice. At lunchtime, Tout Bon offers mixed salads, quiches, soups and simple dishes to suit all tastes (from €9.80 to €11.80), as well as delicious desserts. Quick and efficient service in this Tower of Babel where you'll find mostly Eurocrats.

Mundo Pain

18, rue J. Stas
Metro Louise
☎ 02 537 97 00
Every day 8am-7pm.

A minute's walk from Porte Louise, a new temple to bread, with a fashionable minimalist decor, where you can eat at any time. Delicious homemade

bread, croissants and fresh fruit juice, a small selection of hot dishes for lunch, some interesting wines, mouth-watering pastries, flavored teas, comfy armchairs and beautiful people. What more could you wish for?

La Tsampa

109, rue de Livourne
☎ 02 647 03 67
Trams 93-34
(Lesbroussart)
Lunchtime and evening.
Closed Sat. and Sun.
In the art-nouveau district, this is a favorite address for eating good, healthy food in a peaceful setting. The menu is 100 percent vegetarian, the produce is all natural, the cooking healthy and the veranda very pleasant in all seasons, without forgetting the lovely garden in the summer. Varying with each day, the Tsampa dish of the day (€8.90) may be taken with a salad, a starter or a soup.

Sushi Factory

216, avenue Louise
Trams 93-94 (Lesbroussart)
☎ 02 646 20 20
Every day 11am-9.30pm.

Maki, Nigiri, Yakitori, Sashimi, fresh Miso soup: all is fresh and delicious, to be eaten in or taken out for a picnic in the park. The 'Well-Being' menu costs €10.95 and the Light menu €8.95.

Reasonable prices for basic Japanese cuisine.

The House

30, bd de Waterloo
Metro Louise or Porte de Namur
☎ 02 512 97 27
www.t-house.be
Mon.-Fri. 12am-5.30pm,
Sat. 12am-6pm, Sun.
11.30am-4.30pm.

Near the Hilton and the famous fashion houses, a small upscale backroom clad in fuschia-pink shades and light-colored furniture welcomes you for a lunchbreak, a Mariage Frères cup of tea or Sunday brunch. You can enjoy lovely food, smart company, delicious salads (from €13.95 to €16.85), a club sandwich, a risotto or the dish of the day (€15.95). In summer, the large terrace offers a peaceful haven in the middle of the city.

La Crémerie de la Vache

6, rue Jean Stas
Metro Louise
☎ 02 538 28 18
Mon.-Sat. and holidays
8am-7pm.

On the terrace or inside, the atmosphere is friendly. It is a pleasure to meet up for a chat over a tasty breakfast of real *viennoiseries* (croissants, etc.), delicious jams, a salad or a *tartine* (bread and jam). Treat yourself to a cup of flavored tea served with divine tartlets. Whatever the time of day, this *crémerie* (dairy) is always busy with tourists, passers-by, and young executives

Le Cercle des Voyageurs

18, rue des Grands-Carmes
Metro Bourse
☎ 02 514 39 48
www.lecercledesvoyageurs
.com
Every day 11am-11pm
(midnight Fri. and Sat.)
Once you step over the threshold of this 17th-century private mansion, you'll find yourself admiring a decor worthy of imperial India with its palm trees and comfortable club armchairs. This is the meeting place of seasoned travelers and dreamers where you can enjoy – for lunch or evening meal – an exotic cuisine ranging from *antipasti*

1 - La Crémerie de la Vache
2 - Tout bon
3 - Tea for Two
4 - Passiflore

to *moqueca* from Bahia (€8.50) or Brazilian croquettes, or else drink teas from around the world. This is an ideal place to read a book, have a chat, discover a new wine, take salsa classes, plan your next trip in the library or listen to a concert.

AND ALSO

Le Balmoral p. 61
Au Suisse p. 43
Chez Marcel p. 54
Maison Antoine p. 63
L'Ultime Atome p. 65
Le Perroquet p. 53
Oyster bar p. 47
La Tentation p. 45

Tearooms

Passiflore

97, rue du Bailli
Bus 54 or trams 81-82
(Trinité)
☎ 02 538 42 10
Every day 8am-7pm,
weekends 9am-7pm.

Opposite the baroque church, Passiflore is a yellow and blue tearoom with ottomans and glazed earthenware-top tables patronized by the young, who come to eat savory or sweet dishes, drink a capuccino or enjoy a fresh fruit juice.

Tea for Two

394, chée de Waterloo
Trams 91-92
(Ma Campagne)
☎ 02 538 38 96
Tue.-Sat. 11am-6pm,
Sun. 1-6pm.

The main room is very English in style, with two more intimate little rooms, one decorated in blue, the other gilded, where you can drink smoked Chinese tea or try amazing brews flavored with lotus flowers, essence of mandarin or rose petals. Scones, delicious cheesecake and English cakes are available for afternoon tea or Sunday brunch.

Wittamer Café

13, place du Grand-Sablon
Bus 48 (Grand-Sablon)
☎ 02 546 11 11
Tue.-Sun. 9am-6pm.

An annexe of the famous Wittamer cake shop, this new tearoom, decorated in shades of fuschia and chocolate, will entice you to indulge in one of its divine cakes or a homemade ice cream served with a wide range of teas and coffees. You can also have lunch here: selections at the weekend, and dish of the day for €13 (coffee included) during the week.

ALSO

Comptoir Florian p. 64;
Le Framboisier doré
p. 58; Aux délices de
Capoue p. 63.

Practicalities

Opening hours

Shops in Brussels are open 10am-6.30pm Tuesday to Saturday. On Mondays they're generally closed, though some small shops open at 1.30pm. Remember some shops still close for lunch between 12.30 and 1.30pm. These days, more and more shops are opening on Sundays, especially in the tourist areas, Îlot Sacré, Sablon, Marolles and around Place Brugmann. Sunday is also the 'junk shop day.' Ask at Bruxelles-Tourisme for details of markets other than

those held in Place du Jeu-de-Balle and Sablon.

How to pay

The great majority of shops accept credit cards for payments of over €25 especially Visa, Diners, American Express and Eurocard. For other credit or debit cards, it's better to look at the stickers on the door of the shop before going in. Increasingly you will be asked to key your PIN when using a credit card, although sometimes only a simple signature is required.

Eurocheques and traveler's checks are also usually accepted. However, it's always better to use an automatic cash machine to withdraw money in euros directly from your own account than to pay in any kind of foreign currency. Cash is also often the only means of payment at market stalls or junk shops. Whatever the case, ask for your receipt or your bill: it can be useful if one day you wish to resell what you have just bought or to file a claim with your insurance company if you are the victim of a burglary.

Prices

The law obliges all shop-keepers to price individual items. Only market traders and antique dealers are exempt, which means that you may be able to bargain.

SALES

Sales run for a full month twice a year, starting on January 1 and July 1. To find out about special offers and discount sales (store closures and ends of lines), buy a paper called *Vlan*. Remember you won't be able to obtain a refund for sale items, or exchange them.

Department stores and galeries

Brussels has two good department stores. Galeria Inno (111 rue Neuve and 12 avenue Louise) specializes in luxury products and the famous brand names of ready-to-wear clothes, whereas Rob (28 bd de la Woluwe) is a huge

Shipping procedures

If you want to have an item you've bought sent back home, the store may well be able to provide you with the name of a reputable transportation company. If they can't, you'll have to

Customs formalities

There are no customs formalities for EU citizens, provided they can show a receipt proving that duty was paid on the purchase in Belgium. No specific regulations apply to antiques,

delicatessen the size of a supermarket. The most famous of the large *galeries* (Toison d'Or, Porte Louise, Espace Louise) are rapidly losing ground, with the boutiques migrating to more fashionable areas such as Boulevard de Waterloo and Avenue Louise.

Where to shop

No one goes to Avenue de la Toison-d'Or any more. If you want to find the smart stores, you'll have to cross the road to Boulevard de Waterloo and walk down Avenue Louise. Halfway along, you'll find Rue A. Dansaert, which is now the center of cutting-edge fashion in Brussels. And since Armani moved into Sablon, it looks as though the antique shops here will all soon have been replaced by designer outlets.

decide whether you want to send your goods by air, which is quick but expensive, or surface mail, which will take longer but which offers you greater flexibility as far as price is concerned. An insurance premium is automatically included in the transportation price quoted. If you want to have a really valuable item delivered, you should find a specialist company. The following are two such companies:

Art on the Move

Packs up professionally and delivers works of art all over Europe. Furniture depository is also offered. Prices are calculated according to volume.
☎ 02 333 24 11.

Maertens

Door-to-door delivery and storage of artworks.
☎ 02 751 81 91.

as long as you show a certificate of authenticity and a bill made out by the seller. If you're caught in possession of forged documents the goods will be confiscated and you'll have to pay a heavy fine. You may also be charged with receiving stolen goods when you get back home. Those not resident in the EU may be able to get a reimbursment of VAT on larger purchases. To do this ask the vendor for a special form, which you'll have to fill in at the airport or land border.

FINDING YOUR WAY

Next to each address in the Where to stay, Shopping and Going Out sections, we have given details of the nearest Brussels metro, tram or bus station.

Belgian designers

Take advantage of your visit to Brussels to examine the latest creations by Belgian designers, some of whom have now acquired international status. Whether you are looking for chic, timeless, classic or avant-garde, you'll discover there's something affordable for everyone.

Olivier Strelli

72, avenue Louise
Tram 92 (Stéphanie)
☎ 02 512 56 07
Mon.-Sat. 10am-6.30pm.

Olivier Strelli's preferred colors are turquoise and dark red, his favorite fabric is linen. A degree of continuity in the cut means that you can combine elements from the new collections with clothes from the season before. The transparent moiré-effect blazer can be either worn over jeans or a long dress, and the tailored jacket can be swapped for a long, low-cut tunic. There's plenty here for the men, too, including perfectly cut jackets and waistcoats in wonderfully vibrant colors.

Natan

158, avenue Louise
Tram 93-94 (Defacqz)
☎ 02 647 10 01
Mon.-Sat. 10am-6pm.

The window display is minimalist, the prices (which aren't displayed) are not. To enter this magnificent former mansion, you have to display your worthiness and your designer accessories, otherwise you'll be politely shown the door. If you're a fan of black, grey and natural tones, sober lines and well-cut suits, spangled tops and sheath dresses, you should either expect to pay high prices or wait for the sales to begin in January and July.

Martin Margiela

114, rue de Flandre
Metro Sainte-Catherine
☎ 02 223 75 20
Mon.-Sat. 11am-7pm.

It is in this 18th-century house that the second shop in the world displaying the collection by Martin Margiela opened, following the original in Tokyo. This young and talented creator has already produced a women's collection for Hermès. In 'cottage industry' style, from recycled clothes, he creates designs for both men and women. Accessories and shoes also available.

Kaat Tilley

4, galerie du Roi
Metro Gare Centrale
☎ 02 514 07 63
www.kaattilley.com
Mon.-Fri. 10am-6.30pm,
Sat. 10.30am-6.30pm.

If you wish to have a slender figure in the style of medieval or *fin-de-siècle* dresses, then treat yourself to the creations of this Flemish designer. In a skillfully dilapidated décor, the materials are draped, intertwined, superimposed. The skirts are flared, the straps are threadlike and the stitches quite loose. Elastic and fluid fabrics play on transparency. Visit the surprising *robes de mariée* (wedding dresses) department, too.

Johanne Riss

35, place du Nouveau-
Marché-aux-Grains
Bus 63 (Dansaert)

☎ 02 513 09 00
Mon.-Sat. 10.30am-6.30pm.
Johanne Riss lives and works in this large white loft with its small inner garden. It's the place to come and see a line of very feminine garments. You'll find very tight-fitting tapering dresses in Lycra, either very low-cut or with round necks, to wear on their own or with a transparent over-dress and pearls or fabric flowers as accessories. The wedding dresses are designed in the same spirit with embroidered tulle decorations and silk flowers. Allow around €400 for a short dress, €700 for a jacket.

Isabelle Baines

48, rue du Pépin
Metro Porte de Namur
☎ 02 502 13 73
Tue.-Sat. 10.30am-6pm,
Mon. 2pm-6.30pm.
Knitwear of a quality beyond reproach and a perfect cut come from the house of

Isabelle Baines. She does not 'produce' knitwear but creates pullovers with a soul. Made of wool and cotton, her very subtle plain shades vary according to the seasons. These jumpers are ideal for men and women looking for comfort and warmth. A small cardigan will cost you €200 and a short-sleeved jumper €170. An investment you won't regret.

STIJL

Showcase for the big-name designers (p. 43).

74, rue Antoine Dansaert
Bus 63 (Dansaert)
☎ 02 512 03 13
Mon.-Sat.
10.30am-6.30pm.

Christophe Coppens Le Shop

2, rue Léon Lepage
Metro Bourse or Ste-
Catherine
☎ 02 512 77 97
www.christophecoppens.
com
Tue.-Sat. 11am-6pm.

After working for Yves Saint Laurent, Yamamoto and Guy Laroche, for the last twelve years Christophe Coppens has been designing his own eccentric collections of hats, gloves and scarves. He juggles with different materials (paper, straw, lurex, felt, silk, beads and feathers) and colors. He layers frills as in a tutu, puts together silk and organza, and embroiders crazy patterns on

sculpture-like hats. A real joy which changes with each season and you can watch him at work in his workshop by appointment (☎ 02 538 08 13).

Annemie Verbeke

64, rue Antoine Dansaert
Metro Bourse or Ste-
Catherine
☎ 02 646 25 81
Every day except Tue. and
Sun. 11am-6pm.

Renowned for her knitwear, this Belgian stylist offers a complete range of reversible

dresses (from €300 to €500), asymmetric skirts, comfortable slacks, jackets and coats. The lines are simple and beautiful, the materials comfortable and the cuts subtle. Her favorite colors are satin beige and pink, to be worn with tricolor stripes or checks, which can also be found on her new purse collection.

Mademoiselle Lucien

48, rue A. Campenhout
Metro Schuman
☎ 02 343 38 24
Mon.-Wed. 10-12.30am
and 1.30-5.30pm,
Sat. by appointment

Laurent Uyttersprot and Pascal di Pietro Martellini are the designers behind the charming creations at Mademoiselle Lucien. From soft furnishings,

damask cloth and lampas, they create extremely feminine and colorful outfits, bras, corsets and stoles for all ages. Daytime suits can be transformed into evening wear. Everything can be personalized.

Chris Janssens

13, place du Nouveau
Marché-aux-Grains
Metro Bourse or Ste
Catherine
☎ 02 512 29 97
www.chrisjanssens.com
Mon.- Thu. 10.30am-6.30pm,
Fri.-Sat.11am-6.30pm.

Large sofas and flowery wallpaper: you immediately feel at home in the Liv'in boutique of this fashion designer from Anvers. Her creations in sparkling colors and beautiful materials are aimed at active women aged 25 to 60. Chris Janssens offers a complete look that can be rearranged according to the seasons because the cuts are timeless and yet original. Handmade embroideries and paintings and beautiful knits add to the refinement of these affordable clothes (slacks from €160, blouses from €80).

Azniv Afsar

28, rue Léon Lepage
Metro Sainte-Catherine
☎ 02 512 30 96

Mon.-Tue. by appointment,
Wed.-Sat. 11am-6pm.

Azniv Afsar creates very
structured clothes in natural
materials. She likes
asymmetrical shapes and
always chooses very feminine,
close-fitting and low-cut
lines. She occasionally brings
a touch of color by hand-
painting some of her models.
Allow a budget of €250 to
treat yourself to a modern
and comfortable suit.

Jean-Paul Knott
3, rue Léon Lepage
Metro Bourse or Ste
Catherine
☎ **02 514 18 35**
Mon.-Sat. 10am-6.30pm.

From Brussels, trained in New
York, deputy to Yves Saint
Laurent for his haute couture
collections, Jean-Paul Knott
now creates his own designs.
A great traveler, he designs
clothes for men and women
according to the concept of the
'ideal suitcase'. In black, white,
navy and off-white, made out
of beautiful seasonal materials
(from flannel to satin crepe),
pants, trench coats, shirts,
dressing gowns and dresses all
have a perfect cut, enhanced
with a leather trim. An elegance
which comes at a price: flannel
skirt at €423, long cotton
canvas jacket at €626.

Chine
2, rue Van Artevelde
Metro Bourse
☎ **02 503 14 99**
Mon.-Sat. 11am-6.30pm.

Guillaume Thys has a passion
for silk and his collections are
based on influences from
China where his favorite
material was discovered. His
silk comes in every form:
woven, knitted, crocheted,
pleated, moiré, embroidered
or beaded, and he also uses
voile, jersey, crepe and taffeta.
Elegant, fluid clothes to please
any woman from the youngest
to the more mature. A range of
jeans completes the collection.
Allow up to €250 for a dress.

Serica
19, rue Jean Stas
Metro Louise
☎ **02 534 38 33**
www.serica.be
Mon.-Sat. 10am-6pm.

If the creations of Belgian
fashion designers are a little
over your budget and if you
have golden fingers, here you'll
find all the haute couture
materials you have been
dreaming about. A vast choice
of lace, Italian silks (Valentino,
Ungaro, Armani), Belgian
linens and designer wools. This
shop is always at the forefront
of fashion and well known
among Brussels designers.

BELGIAN FASHION
In 1986, the 'Anvers six', Dries van Noten, Dirk
Bikkembergs, Marina Yee, Dirk Van Saene, Ann
Demeulemeester and Walter Beirendonck, made the
front page of the fashion press by exhibiting their
eccentric creations for the first time in London. If
20 years later their collections have become tamer,
they still have a loyal following, both in Anvers and in
Brussels. During the week of ready-to-wear fashion
shows in Paris, Belgian stylists stand out through their
unbridled imagination coupled with a touch of surrealism.
To discover them live, follow the designers' trail organized
in the Dansaert district by Modo Bruxellae. It takes place
on the last weekend in October every even year.
Information: ☎ 02 502 52 64 – www.modobruxellae.be

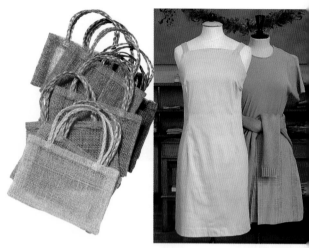

Women's fashion

High fashion isn't only French or Italian. In Brussels' stores you'll find everything: elegance, timelessness, unique items and designer creations, clothes that are trendy, sensible or just downright extravagant. Something for every woman between the ages of 12 and 70, whatever their budget. And some shops now open on Sundays, too.

Nicolas Woit

80, rue Antoine Dansaert
Metro Bourse or Ste
Catherine; ☎ 02 503 48 32
www.nicolaswoit.com
Tue.-Sat. 10.30am-6pm.

Women who want to escape the constraints of fashion and those who love historical garb will adore the unconventional creations of this designer trained in Paris. The luxurious fabrics, daring cuts of suits and dresses for special occasions, highly unusual accessories and new items arriving every two weeks will seduce many a shopper. Evening dresses from around €300.

Rue Blanche

39-41, rue Antoine Dansaert
Metro Bourse

☎ 02 512 03 14
Mon.-Sat. 11am-6.30pm.

Subdued colors and elegant, impeccably cut clothes to flatter the shape of your body. From the very formal to sportswear, all kinds of combinations are possible. You can dress from head to toe in the Rue Blanche brand, including the hat and the eau de toilette.

Mariella Burani

29, rue de Namur
Metro Porte de Namur
☎ 02 514 08 85
Mon.-Sat. 10.30am-6.30pm

Extremely feminine Italian fashions, well-finished and made in fabrics that are comfortable to wear. Combinations of printed designs, reversible jackets and dresses, short or long lines, fur-lined coats, chiffons, all with the same freshness and fluidity, winter or summer

of course these qualities
aren't cheap: around €347
for a dress; around €175 for
a pair of slacks.

La Belle et la Bête

3, rue A.-Dansaert
Metro Bourse
☎ 02 502 66 16
Mon.-Sat. 11am-7pm.

This is the place to find smart
clothes with a little touch of
originality. They are well cut
from good quality material
and the colors are quietly
sensible, as are the flowery
prints of the dresses, blouses
and scarves. You won't have
to wait for the sales to afford
the clothes, either, as the
prices are very reasonable
(suits/slacks at €248, knitted
tops at €75).

Utikii

8, rue de l'Hôpital
Bus 48 (Saint Jean)
☎ 02 513 91 00
Mon.-Sat. 10am-6pm.

In this store with a pale wood
interior you'll find labels from
Scandinavia (Marco Polo,
Granella), Holland (Turnover,
Sandwich) and Belgium
(Waxx), all of whom make
clothes for women who aren't
shaped like supermodels and
loathe close-fitting outfits.
Well-cut clothes in cotton,
wool and linen will make

you feel great. Excellent value
for money has brought this
shop a clientele that's
remained loyal for 25 years.

Peau d'âne

37, rue des Éperonniers
Metro Gare Centrale
☎ 02 513 84 37

HATSHOE

The only boutique where you can find designer Dries Van
Noten shoes as well as styles by other Belgian
designers (Véronique Branquinho, Nathalie Verlinden).
The ideal address to find the yellow pumps and bright
green sandals seen on the feet of catwalk fashion
models. Very trendy, quite expensive (€200 to €500)
but undeniable quality.
89, rue Antoine Dansaert
Metro Bourse or Ste Catherine – ☎ 02 512 41 52
Mon. 12.30-6.30pm, Tue.-Sat. 10.30am-6.30pm.

Every day 11am-7pm,
Fri.-Sat. until 9.30pm.

High fashion at low prices.
Such would be the motto of
Ilana, the designer of tailor-
made clothes in the material of
your choice. In the store, you'll
find basic designs inspired by
the trends of the season, along
with fun accessories. Fitted
jackets over an off-the-
shoulder dress, fake leopard
coats (€145), evening dresses,
long-collared blouses, trousers
(from €50 to €70), and more.
If you can't find anything you
like, place an order: it'll take
about a week to renew your
wardrobe at a reasonable cost.

Zoë

12, rue des Riches-Claires
Metro Bourse
☎ 02 511 41 12
Mon.-Sat. 10.30am-7pm.

This is the shop for 15 to 30
year olds who want to be one
step ahead and acquire the
designs that will become all
the rage. Nothing but good
brands: Sessùn, Frankin &
Marshall, Loreak Mendian
and Formol clothes, Replay
jeans, Freitag belts and
purses. You can find T-shirts
from €30, trousers from
€80 to €100.

Accessories: purses, gloves and jewelry

No matter where you buy your clothes from, you can always add to an outfit with an eye-catching designer scarf or an interesting piece of jewelry. The secret is in the detail. So why not invest in a beautiful pair of leather gloves or a fashionable purse?

Laurent Fontainas

19-21, rue du Rempart-des-Moines
Metro Ste Catherine
☎ **02 218 89 31**
Tue.-Sat. 11am-7pm.

This is a name to remember, guaranteeing the quality of his creations. Craftsman jeweler by trade, Laurent Fontainas is blessed with talent and ideas for startling items of jewelry that cleverly mix different materials – silver, wood, precious and semi-precious stones, and zebu horn. The results are surprising: a wide belt made of horn and leather, a ring cut out of a raw garnet, a ball of shimmering quartz set

inside a wooden ring. Prices, ranging from €50 to €1,000 are very reasonable when you consider that the famous Belgian fashion designers order accessories for their catwalk shows from him.

Sabine Herman

86, rue Faider
Tram 81/82 (Trinité)
☎ **02 640 72 53**
Every day except Sun. and Wed. 12-6pm.

Sabine Herman, a goldsmith who trained in Anvers, creates unique items of jewelry that can change according to your mood and clothes. She plays upon the natural beauty of materials – fresh-water beads, rock crystal, carnelian, along with gold and silver – to create rings, necklaces and earrings (from

€240). Some hand-crafted items by other designers (Sofie Lachaert, Nilton Cunha, Georges Larondelle) can also be found, with fabulous items made out of wood, paper, silver and glass paste from €35.

Christa Reniers

29, rue Antoine Dansaert
Metro Bourse
☎ 02 510 06 60
Mon.-Sat. 10.30am-1pm and 2-6.30pm.

Globes, anemones, ears of corn, leaves, meteors and the sun, all carved in wax before being cast in solid silver or gold. Shapes of a simple beauty and perfect balance that can be worn as pendants, earrings or bands.

Annick Tapernoux

28, rue du Vieux-Marché-aux-Grains
Metro Bourse
☎ 02 512 43 79
Thu.-Sat. 11am-6pm.

Annick Tapernoux is a goldsmith and her favorite material is silver. She plays with surfaces, which are sometimes smooth or brushed, sometimes mat or hammered. She creates items on a circular theme, using this pure shape to produce splendid rings and bracelets. Brushed silver rings start at €90.

Les Précieuses

83, rue Antoine Dansaert
Metro Bourse or Ste Catherine
☎ 02 503 28 98
Mon.-Sat. except Tue. 11am-6.30pm.

Like an old-fashioned boudoir, Les Précieuses jealously hides its accessories for men and women. Forget diamonds and enjoy fashion jewelry made from glass beads for the tidy sum of €100! And what about socks, scarves and Antipast gloves or baroque Jamin Puech purses? Refined accessories for princes and princesses.

Timeless

142A, avenue Louise
Tram 94 (Defacqz)
☎ 02 648 45 52
Tue.-Fri. 1.30-6.30pm.

Very valuable and expensive jewelry. A fine range of 20th-century gold and silver pieces and costume jewelry, with many art-nouveau, art-deco, 1960s and 1970s pieces as well as contemporary Scandinavian designs. Among the treasures you'll find beautiful purses and scarves and vintage garments.

Ganterie italienne

3, galerie de la Reine
Metro Gare Centrale
☎ 02 512 75 38
Mon.-Sat. 10am-12.30pm and 1.30-6pm, closed Mon. May-Oct.

Founded in 1890, this is one of those old-fashioned shops where you feel like lingering and trying on handfuls of gloves just for the pleasure of seeing the pairs in hand-stitched peccary skin, kid, silk-lined lambskin and sheepskin emerging from the drawers. It'll certainly put you off all those woolen gloves you find in department stores. A pair from here is €50 on average. Peccary skin is rarer and therefore more expensive.

Delvaux

27, boulevard de Waterloo
Metro Louise
31, galerie de la Reine
Metro Gare Centrale
☎ 02 513 05 02
Mon.-Sat. 10am-6.30pm.

True excellence from this company, who have been producing purses made entirely by hand, including fastenings and metal buckles, since 1829. Besides their enormous creativity (30 to 40 new styles every year), Delvaux design a multitude of accessories, from key rings to motorcycle helmets, covered in tawny leather to match the silk scarves.

HOW TO GIVE YOUR SILVER JEWELRY ITS SHINE BACK

Lay out your jewelry on a piece of aluminum foil in a glass bowl. Sprinkle it with salt, pour on boiling water and let it stand for a few minutes. The result is absolutely amazing, and you don't have to do any rubbing!

Men's
fashion

There's nothing like spending a weekend abroad to remind you it's high time you bought yourself some new clothes. Not that the prices here are necessarily better than you'll find at home, but for once you'll actually have the time to try on a new pair of designer trousers and perhaps a Paul Smith shirt, which will give you a totally new look. And don't miss the creations by Martin Margiela, Jean-Paul Knott and Xavier Delcour.

Balthazar

22, rue du Marché-aux-Fromages
Metro Gare Centrale
☎ 02 514 23 96
Mon.-Sat. 11am-6.30pm.

For stylish men's fashions make your way to this charming 17th-century

building a stone's throw from Grand-Place, in a street full of pizza and kebab stores. These garments with Paul Smith, Smedley and Naessens labels are designed for active men who follow fashion. The cut, fabric and color are important, with the details making all the difference, from colored buttons to accessories. Items aren't extravagantly priced, but they aren't within the range of every budget (polo shirts between €50 and €80, suits around €650).

Christophe Coppens Man

2, rue Léon Lepage; Metro Bourse or Ste-Catherine
☎ 02 512 77 97
Tue.-Sat. 11am-6pm.

Whether you are the rebellious type or a refined gentleman, you'll find a hat to suit you from this Belgian hatter, who inaugurated his men's collection in 2005. Sober and pure materials with eye-catching details such as a light blue bowler hat adorned with bows. You'll also find original accessories, such as pirate scarves and sailor neckerchiefs as well as more classical silk scarves and ties. A natural straw hat costs €175, a tie €58.

Jacques Smadja

21, avenue Louis Lepoutre
Bus 60 (Tenbosch)
☎ 02 346 50 13
Mon.-Sat. 11am-6.30pm.

The lair of a master dresser of elegant, fashionable men.

A man with perfect taste, Jacques Smadja has selected a range of distinctive clothes from the best designers, in particular the wonderful sweaters by Isabelle Baines (see p. 95).

Parachute Jump

579, chaussée de Waterloo
Bus 60 (Tenbosch)
☎ **02 347 49 84**
Mon.-Sat. 10am-6.30pm.

This sportswear center is mainly frequented by women searching for that special gift. The former hardware store with its ostentatious displays is very well stocked, winter and summer, with shirts of every color, unusual ties and thousands of accessories for men who want to impress.

Centre-ville

63, rue des Éperonniers
Metro Gare Centrale
☎ **02 502 27 04**
Mon.-Sat. 11am-6pm,
Sun. 12h-17h.
In this tiny shop, you'll find nothing but Irié designs, a line of extremely well-cut clothes acclaimed by *Marie-Claire* and *Elle*. In black, white and metal grey, jackets, trousers, shirts and polo shirts are cut from sober fabrics (cotton, viscose, acetate), all machine-washable. Essentials, but they come at a price: €698 for a

suit, €182 to €230 for a pair of trousers, €298 for a short jacket and €185 for a leather weekend travel bag.

Bishop Tailors

53b, quai de Mariemont
Bus 63 (Duchesse)
☎ **02 515 00 55**
www.bishop-tailors.be
Mon.-Thu. 9am-4pm,
Fri. 9am-3pm.

Near Place du Grand-Sablon, Bishop Tailors offers the elegance of a made-to-measure suit. Cut to English or Italian style, you can choose from a wide range of fabrics and, especially, designs. Jackets, trousers, shirts, coats and accessories all represent good quality at affordable prices. A tailor-made shirt starts from €93 and a suit from €643.

Degand Sport

4, rue Saint-Georges
Tram 94 (Abbaye)
☎ **02 649 23 00**
Mon.-Sat. 10am-6.30pm.

A sports department has just been opened at the back of this great made-to-measure specialist. Here you'll find a range of comfortable, tasteful clothes for active men who like to be elegant whatever they're doing. You can have a yellow check linen jacket or a

choice of trousers, cotton sweaters and denim shirts to go with your Tods. The prices are pretty much top-of-the-range, too.

Allen Edmonds

223, galerie Louise
Metro Louise
☎ **02 511 35 63**
Mon.-Sat. 10.30am-6.30pm.

Nothing but beautiful American all-leather shoes coming in different versions: town shoes, moccasins or ankle boots. A good alternative to Church shoes, since these are a little less expensive (€200 to €470) and just as durable. You can also find genuine Sebago Docksides.

THE RETURN OF THE DANDY

Are you up with the latest styles? Shoulders should be narrow, waists and armholes close-fitting with big turn-ups on the trousers. Fabrics are now brighter and more colorful. No worries these days about using synthetic and natural fibers that are blended to create elasticity and a *moiré* effect.

Children's
clothes, shoes and toys

Whether you're sold on frilly pink layettes and smocks or prefer a more fashionable look to make your child stand out from the crowd, you'll be spoiled for choice in the many stores for children. Belgian designs don't get exported that much, so your purchases are guaranteed to make heads turn back home. When it comes to toy stores, there's really no reason at all why they should be just for children!

Kat en Muis

32, rue Antoine Dansaert
Metro Bourse
☎ **02 514 32 34**
Mon.-Sat. 10.30am-6.30pm.

Here you'll find Max et Lola, Anne Kurris and Garçon in miniaturized versions adapted to suit children from 3 months to 16 years. Top of the range means top prices, but given the enormous choice, you can easily combine styles and prices to suit yourself, for example a basic T-shirt with designer pants.

Boucle d'Or

12, rue Tabellion
Trams 81-82 (Trinité)
☎ **02 649 96 39**
Tue.-Sat. 11am-6pm.

Because she fancied colors other than the eternal baby blue and pink, Sabrina Palmisano created her own collection of clothes and house linen for small children (0 to 6 years). Three cheers for the fuchsia-pink bodysuit, bright orange duvets, alpaca sweaters and bright-colored bibs! Be warned:

you are bound to fall in love with such things as tea sets, wooden toys, fluffy animals, 'haute couture' boxes, as well as favorite DVDs and CDs. A very personal universe where you'll find a warm welcome.

Claude Hontoir

14, place Brugmann
Bus 60 (Brugmann)
☎ **02 346 59 47**
www.claudehontoir.com
Mon.-Sat. 11am-6pm,
Sun. 11am-4pm.

This designer favors punchy colors and practical, comfortable styles. Pretty dresses and matching Alice bands for girls; for boys: jeans, pants, eye-catching jumpers and check shirts. Expect to pay around €60 for a 6-month-old baby's outfit. There's also a new section for games, toys, nightwear and furniture.

Basile & Boniface

77, rue de Washington
Trams 93-94 (Vleurgat)
☎ 02 534 81 18
Mon. 2-6.30pm, Tue.-Sat.
10.30am-6.30pm.

Are you looking for a fashionable baby hat, a little sporty raincoat, a tiny fleece, an unusual sweater or a frilly little dress? Basile dresses toddlers up to 4 years old and is not afraid of using bright colors.

The GrassHoper

39-43, rue du Marché-aux-Herbes
Metro Bourse
☎ 02 511 96 22
Every day 10am-7pm.

Over two floors, you'll find everything for tiny babies and older children: bath toys, crocodile-shaped flannels, cuddly toys, of course, but also puzzles and new versions of traditional toys. It is a real joy to get lost in here.

Tinok

165, avenue Louise
Tram 93-94 Defacqz)
☎ 02 646 35 87
Mon.-Sat. 10.30am-6.30pm.

In this huge space, you'll find everything from the 'maternity' suitcase to Dior

MUSÉE DU JOUET

A journey through the history of toys. Among the attractions is a puppet show in a room with a reconstruction of an historic Brussels tram. Reproductions of old mechanical toys and games from all over the world are also on sale (from €3.50 to €300).
24, rue de l'Association
Metro Botanique or
Madou; ☎ 02 219 61 68
Every day 10-12am,
2-6pm.

and Burberry christening gowns. If the hand-stitched I Pinco Pallino 2 piece set (from €200) is not on your list of priorities, you cannot fail to fall in love with the old-fashioned toys and the more modern ones (rocking horse €160), baby cameras, very useful travel cots (€420) and three-wheeled pushchairs. You'll also love the *bola mexicana* (€20), a small musical ball to put on the future mum's stomach to help the baby dance!

Noukie's Store

70, avenue Louise
Metro Louise or tram 91-93-94 (Stéphanie)
☎ 02 514 56 63
Mon.-Sat. 10am-6pm.

A wide range of clothes, cuddly animals, soft toys, linen and accessories – plates, baby bottles and activity mats with a new theme each year. Clothes and soft toys are in cotton and mixed cotton and velvet in pastel shades, with a few more colorful seasonal touches. A very wide choice at good prices (sleeping bag for €40, cuddly toys for €26).

Pygmées

4, rue des Grands-Carmes
Metro Bourse
☎ 02 512 27 75
Tue.-Thu. 11am-6.30pm,
Fri.-Sat. 11.30am-7pm.

A line of amusing and colorful clothes for children (from 3 months to 8 years) who like to dress up as little elves and put on face paints. These two well-traveled designers bring back materials and ideas in their suitcases to create fun clothes. Allow €4 for one of these hand-stitched marvels (which also come in adult sizes for parents).

Les Casse-Pieds

571, chaussée de Waterloo
Bus 54 (Ma Campagne)
☎ 02 343 26 68
Mon.-Sat. 10am-6.30pm.

Say goodbye to stiff blue or white shoes, and hello to fashion and colors! A good compromise which will please children and adults alike, as these are small versions of parents' shoes. Here choice and quality prevail.

Interior decoration,
tableware and design

In your visits to some of the city's fashionable restaurants and cafés you'll have noticed that the inhabitants of Brussels are experts at interior design. Their homes are larger than the European average and they love high-class furniture, quality materials and beautiful objects, which they display to great effect. Look carefully, and you will find something that's right for you in almost every shop.

DESIGN

Ligne
12-16, galerie de la Reine
Metro Gare Centrale

☎ 02 511 60 30
Mon.-Sat. 10am-6pm.

You'll find all the great names in contemporary design, from F.L. Wright to Jasper Morrison,

in this magical shop that draws you irresistibly inside. It's been at the cutting edge of style for 30 years, selling top-of-the-range items only. The exclusive outlet for *Woodnotes* carpets, made in Finland from paper cord at around €181 per m² (sq. yd). All items are similarly expensive and beautiful.

In Store
90-92, rue Tenbosch
Tram 94-Vleurgat
☎ 02 344 96 37
Mon.-Fri. 10am-7pm,
Sat. 11am-6pm.

A wonderful showroom with sections for day, night and office, where Italian contemporary design (B&B Italia, Flexform, Max Alto, Knoll, Vitra) takes pride of place. This immense showroom is laid out like a model apartment where pure lines blend with the rigorous layout.

Espace Bizarre

17-19, rue des Chartreux
Metro Bourse
☎ 02 514 52 56
www.espacebizarre.com
Tue.-Sat. 10am-7pm.

This concept store is indelibly Japanese: futons, beautiful lacquered items, pure lines, coffee tables, shoji screens, kimonos and slippers. The designer items displayed here meet the top-of-the-range criteria at affordable prices. Among the Belgian brands worth mentioning are Vlaemsch with their Bootbag and the series Élan + Cerf, and B-products with their beautiful stainless steel furniture. There is a range of lamps and furniture made of solid Dutch wood (Moooi, Birdman), novelty items like Magis draining boards and Vipp dustbins. Don't miss it!

FABRICS

Les Tissus du Sablon

31, rue Joseph Stevens
☎ 02 784 38 64
Bus 48 (Grand-Sablon)
☎ 02 502 48 60
Tue.-Sat. 10am-6pm,
Sun. 11am-3pm.

The ideal address if you wish to re-upholster a Louis XV armchair or find some curtains. This shop offers a generous range of materials fashioned from pure Egyptian cotton. The old-style patterns have been reworked and adapted to modern interiors while still respecting the previous life of the furniture and the room. If you're undecided, you'll always be well advised.

Linen House

10, rue Bodenbroeck
Bus 48 (Grand-Sablon)
☎ 02 502 63 02
Tue.-Sat. 10.30am-12.30pm
and 1.30-6.30pm,
Sun. 10.30am-3pm.

Flemish linen has long had a solid reputation. The robust yet fine fiber makes wonderful tablecloths and clothes. This company, which specializes in linen, sells fabric by the meter in large widths, as well as dishcloths, tablecloths and napkins in standard sizes. You can also order individualized items, including damask, lacy tablecloths or cloths embroidered with your initials. Transportation home of your purchases can also be arranged for you.

Limited Edition

35, rue de Namur
Metro Porte de Namur
☎ 02 512 23 68
www.limitededition.be
Mon.-Sat. 10.30am-6.30pm.

This Belgian shop specializes in bespoke braided rugs made according to traditional techniques. The materials used are all natural – wool and cotton, cotton and silk, linen, sisal, calfskin and leather – dyed in the colors of your choice. From the very exclusive Zebrano, woven suede and leather to the hand-tufted long pile carpets, prices vary from €280 to €378 per m^2 (sq. yd). Allow 5 to 8 weeks for delivery.

HOME DECORATION AND ORNAMENTS

Chintz Shop

35-39, rue de Rollebeek
Bus 48 (Grand-Sablon)
☎ 02 513 58 96
Tue.-Fri. 10am-6pm,
Sat. 10.30am-6pm, Sun.
10.30am-4pm.

The 'shabby chic' style comes direct from LA. You'll be won over by the simplicity and friendly atmosphere of this deliciously old-fashioned store with its faded flower prints and armchairs with frilly cushions. Crystal chandeliers and a few old ornaments add the finishing touches. Owner Amélie de Borchgrave is on hand to help you with decorative, and decorous, advice.

Top-Mouton

71, rue de l'Écuyer
Metro De Brouckère
☎ 02 513 35 99
Tue. and Fri. 11am-7pm
and by appointment.

For three generations, this gallery has been selecting timeless designer items for the home which must match three criteria: functionality, quality and simplicity. This is why you'll find here Scandinavian pieces from the 1940s, as well as creations by contemporary Belgian designers. A place to worth investigating.

Emery & Cie

25-29, rue de l'Hôpital
Bus 48, 95 or 96
(Saint-Jean)
☎ 02 513 58 92
Mon.-Sat. 11am-7pm.

If you loved the set of the Mozart film *Amadeus*, then make for the three floors of this magnificent old building. The rooms are decorated in shades of red, yellow, green dark purple with wrought-iron furniture and lights. They show a fondness for tiles in colored cement or Moroccan *zellige*, and brocade decorated with bees. Emery's strong point is color. Wrought iron accessories (candlesticks, chairs, etc) and Tamgrout crockery designed or selected by Emery and Co. complete the picture. Organdy and voile fabrics are also available from €14 to €16 per m² (sq. yd).

New De Wolf

91, rue Haute/40, rue Blaes
Bus 20 and 48 (Chapelle)
☎ 02 511 10 18
Mon.-Sat. 10am-6.30pm,
Sun. 10am-4pm.

Covering 2,500 m², the home-decoration hypermarket is organized by theme: Africa, Tuscany, Asia, Britain, the beach, the garden, etc. Their stock is constantly renewed, enabling you to make real discoveries and to buy furniture at a reduced price: proof that beautiful things are not always expensive. What's more, goods can be delivered, even to other European countries, provided you have purchased enough furniture.

Baltazar

100, rue de Stassart
Metro Louise
☎ 02 512 85 13
Tue.-Sat. 10.30am-6.30pm,
Sun. 11am-5pm.

If you'd like to treat yourself to an Alechinsky lithograph, an engraving by Gabriel Belgeonne, Pompon's white bear or a Khmer Buddha's head, well you can! This is the art bazaar where you'll find a mix of resin reproductions of works of art from the great museums and original works by Belgian and foreign artists. For €75 to €6,000, you can buy works that will enhance your home and turn your guests green with envy.

DAM Spazio

13, rue Lepage
Metro Sainte-Catherine
☎ 02 502 99 50
Thu.-Sat. 12-6.30pm
and by appointment

A tiny store window displaying little known (and therefore cheaper) names, designer items and contemporary art. This is where you'll find L'Anverre glass creations, solid wood Danish furniture by Globe, and a few special pieces such as the panels and arrangements by Guido'Lu. Worth noting, too, are the striking handmade tiles.

Flamant

36, pl. du Grand-Sablon
Bus 48 (Grand-Sablon)

A ROYAL BOCH DINNER SERVICE

La Louvière is still making crockery that is highly prized for the quality of its china, a mix of clay and kaolin, with all the solidity of porcelain. The pieces are decorated using transfers, which are sometimes retouched by hand and are permanently fixed by a second firing at 1,140°C. Prices are double for Copenhagen crockery (a design of fine blue lines) and Rangoon (plain with beading). Period pieces are much sought-after.

☎ **02 514 47 07**
Mon.-Thu. 10.30am-6.30pm, Fri. 10.30am-7pm, Sat. 10am-7pm, Sun. 10am-6pm.

The very latest decorative trends are displayed in this vast space, laid out like a house from the leafy suburbs of Brussels or Antwerp. From the lounge to the nursery and the kitchen, with the latest equipment, some good decorating ideas, luxurious though impractical items, very classy sofas. One of Princess Mathilda's favorite addresses.

TABLEWARE

Villeroy et Boch

37, avenue Louise
Metro Louise
☎ **533 10 51**
www.villeroy-boch.com
Mon.-Sat. 10am-6pm.
China and earthenware by this venerable Luxembourg firm founded in 1748 are not only hardwearing but also very beautiful and varied. Here you'll find everything you could dream of to lay out your table beautifully, as well as little accessories to brighten up daily life, such as a Fore kettle (€30), a designer Thermos flask (€35) or children's cutlery sets (€19).

Dille & Kamille

16, rue Jean-Stas
Metro Louise
☎ **538 81 25**
Mon.-Sat. 9.30am-6.30pm.

As soon as the sun comes out, the pavement is covered in pots full of sunflowers and aromatic herbs, giving you a hint of the fragrances to be enjoyed in this wonderful store

specializing in cooking utensils. Iron, wooden or stainless steel spoons, lemon squeezers, ice-cream servers, strawberry hullers, dozens of cake tins of different shapes, picnic hampers, spices, teas and jams – all at prices to confound the competition.

Argus Corp

11, rue van Moer
Tram 92/93/94 (Petit-Sablon)
☎ **02 511 28 35**
Tue.-Sat. 11am-noon and 2-5pm, Sun. 11am-1pm.

Superb cut crystal glasses by Val Saint Lambert dating from 1900 to 1950. Here you can replace the ones you've broken or buy a complete set at half price. If your dinner guests are on the clumsy side this store is the answer to your prayers. You'll also find pieces by Gallé, Daum and Lalique.

Sweet treats

In Brussels it's traditional to take a *ballotin* of pralines (a box of chocolates) as a gift when you're invited to someone's house. So you know what you will be giving, here are some places you can be sure of finding the best products in the city at prices distinctly lower than those you'll pay elsewhere. Don't forget that chocolates generally travel well.

Neuhaus

25-27, galerie de la Reine
Metro Gare Centrale
☎ 02 512 63 59
Mon.-Sat. 10am-8pm,
Sun. 10am-7pm.

The inventor of the concept of the *ballotin* and of the name 'praline' is one of the oldest Belgian chocolate manufacturers. His best-known products are *caprice* and *tentation* ('temptation'),

which are nougatines filled with fresh cream. Success has led to the opening of several further outlets in key locations throughout the city. The price per kilo of his delicious pralines is a lot less than elsewhere (around €34).

Corné Toison d'Or

24-26, galerie du Roi
Metro Gare Centrale or
De Brouckère
☎ 02 512 49 84
Every day 10am-7pm.

For a real treat ask for an assortment of *mendiants* – chocolate with dried fruit and almonds – and *florentines*, biscuits with almonds, honey

and very dark chocolate. Then throw in a few sugar-coated

pralines or marzipan *manons*. These delicious chocolates cost around €39 per kg.

Mary

73, rue Royale
Metro Madou
☎ 02 217 45 00
Mon.-Sat. 9.30am-6pm.

This chocolate supplier to the royal family, located opposite the Congress column, is now in the hands of the third generation, with the wife selling the produce made by her husband. Everything is done by hand, including whipping the cream. Blue and gold decor and very dark chocolate is used, ranging from very sweet to bitter with 99.7 percent cocoa. While a less fatty milk chocolate than usual is tolerated, white chocolate is banned. There are handy cool bags to hold the chocolates, which are several times the price of their mass-produced rivals (€46 per kg), but incomparably better.

Irsi

15, rue du Bailli
Trams 93-94 (Lesbroussart)
☎ **02 648 70 50**
Mon.-Sat. 8.45am-6.30pm.

An old-fashioned confectioner's with rows of jars full of *manons* – sweets covered in white chocolate and filled with fresh cream. *Manons* come in various flavors: vanilla, mocha, Grand Marnier, cognac and Napoleon Mandarin. Other specialties include less rich fruit creams and *orangettes* (chocolate with orange). A kilo of chocolates will cost you €32, a kilo of fruit creams €24.

Planète Chocolat

24, rue du Lombard
Metro Anneessens
☎ **02 511 07 55**
Tue.-Sat. 10am-6.30pm,
Sun. 11am-6pm.

At Emmanuel Bussels, a master chocolate maker who creates his pralines in front of you in made-to-measure molds, you can crunch the

front of one of the buildings around Grand-Place, a gothic church or a work of art.

Needless to say, this sweet-toothed gourmet only uses the best quality products to create his ephemeral works of art or to serve you a delicious hot chocolate in his tea room.

De Boe

36, rue de Flandre
Metro Sainte-Catherine
☎ **02 511 13 73**
Tue.-Sat. 9am-6pm.

The De Boe taste has been passed down from generation to generation, from great-grandfather Cyrille, who first opened his roasting business in 1896. The machine is still in action every morning, giving off the lovely aroma of pure arabica coffee. You'll also find blended teas, green tea with cardamom, cornflower tea, and many other delicious things, including Valrhona chocolate, *tartuffo* and capers with sea salt.

A ROMAN TRADITION

Pliny the Elder noted that good children were rewarded with gifts of cakes made of flour and honey in the shape of gods from the Roman Pantheon. It was almost certainly Roman legionnaires who introduced these treats into Gaul, where they still bring joy to children. On the eve of December 6, St Nicholas' day, slippers are hung by every chimney, waiting to be filled with sweets in exchange for a few carrots for the saint's donkey. Of course they're only given to good children!

Pierre Marcolini

1, rue des Minimes
Bus 48 (Grand-Sablon)
☎ **02 514 12 06**
Fri.-Sat. 9am-8pm,
Sun.-Thu. 10am-7pm.

Venezuela, Ghana, Trinity, Chuao, Java, Madagascar, Ecuador, here you can discover the great vintages of plain chocolate at the best chocolate maker's in Belgium. Irresistible at €54 per kilo, wrapped in elegant black boxes (see p. 11).

Dandoy

31, rue au Beurre
Metro Bourse
☎ **02 511 03 26; Mon.-Sat.**
8.30am-6.30pm, Sun. and
holidays 10.30am-6.30pm.
Belgium's oldest biscuit-maker, where all the products are made by hand. Hard to choose between the *speculoos*, *massepain*, *pain à la grecque* and *pain d'épices*. As for the *couques de Dinant* they are used as kitchen decorations

and can be eaten all the year round.

Garcia

75, avenue de la Couronne
Trams 81-82 (Germoir)
☎ **02 640 79 56**
Every day except Fri.
7.30am-6pm; closed 3pm
Sun.

Azulejos, colorful stained-glass windows and a lot of people queueing. You'll have guessed you are in a Portuguese bakery and cake shop. Try the divine *pasteis*, pastries made with egg custard.

It's raining presents

Models of Tintin or Mannekenpis aren't the only souvenirs you can take home with you from this city with its true passion for objects. From the weird to the wonderful, exotic or amusing, here are some addresses where you can find an original present for yourself or a friend.

Dans la presse ce jour-là

64-66, rue des Commerçants
Metro Yser
☎ 02 511 43 89
www.press-and-birthday.com
Mon.-Fri. 11.30am-6.30pm.

If you'd like to know what was happening in the world on the day you were born, why not buy a Belgian newspaper? For friends a bottle of port or Armagnac produced the year they were born will always make a welcome gift. Of course it's better for your wallet if none of the recipients are centenarians! Or what about a family album, a hand-bound book for documents and photographs of life's important moments.

Z'Art

40, rue des Pierres
Metro Bourse
☎ 02 502 61 21
Mon.-Sat. 11am-7pm.

Magritte and Picabia would have loved these objects, whose shape bears no relation to their function. The cow is a bath plug, the tie is made of latex, the clock is in the shape of a flowery lawn or a French fry, the lamps are made of papier

mâché. Everything is surprising, colorful and useful. Lots of ideas for amusing presents from €1 to €250.

La Boutique Tintin

13, rue de la Colline
Metro Gare Centrale
☎ 02 514 51 52
Mon.-Sat. 10am-6pm, Sun. and holidays 11am-5pm.

Even if you're not a fan of the little reporter and his faithful dog, Snowy, you'll find a few original items here, in particular a new ready-to-wear collection and accessories. Little pyjamas with an embroidered Tintin and Snowy for €39, polo shirts from €20, ties, socks and watches, all decorated with the adventures of our hero.

Brussels Corner

27, rue de l'Étuve
Metro Bourse
☎ 02 511 98 49
Every day 10am-7pm winter, 9am-10.30pm summer.

Do you fancy buying a Mannekenpis to uncork your

bottles? If you must buy the traditional souvenir, then you might as well make use of it – and have you actually seen the statue of this little boy relieving himself on a street corner?

Matière Première

52, rue du Bailli
Bus 54 (Trinité)
☎ **02 502 02 30**
Mon.-Sat. 11am-6.30pm.

This whole shop is centered around color. There is a blue monochrome corner, a yellow one, a green one and a dark purple one. In each of the corners are candles, perfumes, incense sticks, paper napkins, organdy table mats – a thousand items for the home, a thousand ideas for colorful presents at low prices.

Nénuph'Art

147, chaussée de Wavre
Bus 34-80 (Parnasse)
☎ **02 512 11 39**
10.15am-6pm except Wed.
and Sun.
Beads of glass, crystal, stone, shells, *millefiori* and silver; beads from Bohemia, Murano, Africa, Asia and elsewhere. There are more than 5,000 varieties of multicolored beads, new and old. Enough to inspire you to create your own jewelry fit for a queen. And to please your friends when you return, have a look at the bead kits starting at €7.

Bougie Gommers

994, chaussée de Waterloo
Bus 365, W or 41 (Vert-
Chasseur)
☎ **02 375 34 38**
Tue.-Fri. 10am-6pm,
Sat. 10am-3pm.

Happily the arrival of electricity hasn't affected the business of this family, who've

Nénuph'Art

been working in wax since 1893. In this little shop you'll find a candle for every occasion, from church candles to candles in the shape of Easter eggs, star signs, cauliflowers, champagne bottles, Buddhas as well as souvenir candles in the shape of a beer mug, a Brussels' paving stone and, of course, Mannekenpis.

Zigzag 123

103, boulevard Anspach
Metro Bourse
☎ **02 512 31 03**
Mon.-Sat. 10am-6.30pm.

The concept is Danish: all the items cost €1, €2 or €3. To the scented candles, photograph frames and soaps which form the permanent

stock, are added, according to weekly deliveries, toys, espresso or cappuccino cups, kitchen and bathroom utensils, paper napkins, violet candies, etc. In short, a place to buy presents without spending a fortune.

ALSO

Rosalie Pompon
1, rue de l'Hôpital – ☎ 02 512 35 93
Mon. 2pm-6.30pm, Tue.-Sun. 10.30am-6.30pm.
Furniture made of papier mâché, eccentric gadgets, fairy lights and countless novelty objects.

La Boîte à Musique
74, Coudenberg – ☎ 02 513 09 65
Mon.-Sat. 9.30am-6.30pm.
The only music shop in the city specializing in classical music. More than 30,000 titles and an independent record company, Pavane Records.

Also **100 % Design**, the king of inflatables (see p. 47); the 1001 treasures of Violaine at **Graphie sud** (see p. 61); **Plaizier**, original postcards (see p. 41).

Antiques

Anyone will tell you that Brussels is one of the hubs of the antiques world. The sales rooms are packed with foreign buyers, so make sure you do the rounds of the antiques stores and don't hesitate to ask the price of an item if it isn't displayed. The dealers' secret lies in the city's low rents and a very high turnover, which means they're always renewing their stock.

Au fil du temps

41, rue Lebeau
Bus 34/48 (Grand-Sablon)
☎ **02 513 34 87**
Every day 2-6pm or by
appointment.

A good place to find high-quality 19th-century bronzes: Carpeaux and, if you're lucky, maybe even a Rodin. Berkowitsch also specializes in period Boch ceramics and Austrian furniture from the early years of the 20th century.

Ciel mes bijoux

16, galerie du Roi
Metro Gare Centrale
☎ **02 514 71 98**
Tue.-Sat. 11am-6pm.

Patrick and Godelieve Sigal have specialized for 22 years in high-class jewelry. In their

smart store, designer collections and a luxurious choice of unique antique pieces are presented, most of them signed by the great names in haute couture from the 1930s to the present – Chanel, Schiaparelli, Dior, Balenciaga, etc. Baroque and semi-precious jewels with wide ranging prices.

Atmosphères

17, rue de Rollebeek
Bus 48 (Grand-Sablon)
☎ **02 513 11 10**
Tue.-Sat.11am-6pm,
Sun. 11am-2pm.

If you feel nostalgic for the colonial era and love 19th-century French and English furniture, make sure you visit this dealer, who buys only what he likes himself. Indian

lanterns hanging from the ceiling, portraits and hunting trophies on the walls and, dotted around on the furniture, numerous ornaments and unusual objects that would look perfect in your home.

Faisons un rêve

112, avenue Lepoutre
Bus 60 (Brugmann)
☎ **02 347 34 29**
Tue.-Wed. 2pm-6.30pm,
Thu.-Sat. 11am-6.30pm,
Sun. 11am-3pm.

Raymond de Bessel is one of those characters who cultivate the love of the beautiful.

Specializing in the1950s and 1960s, he hunts around for the most beautiful Scandinavian jewelry (Georg Jensen, Hans Hansen,Penti Sarpa Neva), Italian lights (Fontana Arte, Mazzega), Scandinavian glassware (Ernest Gordon) and furniture from the Art déco period to the 1960s. The dream

comes to fruition when he holds outstanding exhibitions of a present-day goldsmith or photographer.

Orient Antiques

11-13, quai au Bois-à-Brûler
Metro Sainte-Catherine
☎ **02 511 27 11**
www.orient-antiques.be
Mon.-Fri. 1.30-5.30pm,
Sat. 11am-6pm and by
appointment.

This dealer is rightly renowned for his professionalism. The furniture he displays in his shop is Japanese or Chinese, the statues and ethnic artifacts from Africa, Oceania and South-East Asia. Everything is magnificent and expensive (large Chinese wardrobes from €2,400 to €3,100) but authenticity is guaranteed. You can also treat the gallery like a museum, as there is an explanatory card identifying every item. If you can't afford to buy, you can still educate yourself while admiring the beautiful objects.

Anthémion

65, rue Armand
Campenhout Trams 93/94
(Vleurgat)
☎ **02 537 47 94**
Tue.-Sat. 1-6pm.

A large choice of French, Italian, Scandinavian and German furniture from the 18th to the 20th centuries. The inlaid boxes of various origins, ceramics and small curios are worth a special

mention. Take advantage of Daniel Ahrend's sound advice.

Hôtel des ventes Horta

70-74 avenue de Roodebeek
Metro Diamant
☎ **02 741 60 60**
www.horta.be; viewing Fri.
2-8pm, Sat. 10am-7pm,
Sun. 10am-6.30pm (Mon.
and Tue. to 7.30pm except
Jul.-Aug.)

Find out the viewing dates for the monthly sale before you plan your weekend. If you can't make the sale itself, you can send in a written order or arrange for a telephone line. You need to add 20 percent in charges to the auction price, and possibly 3–6 percent additional fees for a sculpture or painting. If you have access to the internet, you can view an image of the object.

Salle des ventes des Beaux-Arts

40, place du Grand-Sablon
☎ **02 504 80 30**
www.servarts.be
Viewing Fri.-Sat. 10am-
6pm. Sales Tue., Wed. and
Thu. at 2pm.

The oldest auction room in Belgium (1933) moved in 2004 to the very heart of the antiques district. Two of the sales organized here every two months are devoted to Belgian art (May and December).

ASIAN FURNITURE: THE RIGHT PRICE

You'll no doubt be amazed to find the Chinese wardrobe you saw in a reputable dealer's shop sold at a quarter or fifth of the price by another trader. You need to remember that the price of Asian furniture largely depends on the wood it's made from, with sandalwood the most valuable and pine the least. Next in importance comes the age of the piece and last but not least, the quality of the restoration. A piece of furniture that's been left in damp conditions may well split in a dry, heated environment if it hasn't been treated properly.

Vintage
and secondhand

If you've been foolish enough to throw away all your old clothes from the 1970s, don't panic! There are loads of places specializing in flared jeans, platform shoes and check pants. However, if it's a classic item you're after, such as a fur coat or a Chanel suit, you'll find these are also available in the classier secondhand shops.

Modes

164, rue Blaes
Bus 20-48 (Jeu-de-Balle)
☎ **02 512 49 07**
Tue.-Fri. 10am-2.30pm,
Sat.-Sun. 10am-3.30pm.

Here you'll meet movie wardrobe masters and designers looking for inspiration. All the clothes and accessories are pre-1950s and in very good condition. The ideal address to find a complete old-fashioned *trousseau*, a felt *borsalino*, a 1930s polka dot ballgown and strass jewelry.

Look 50

10, rue de la Paix
Metro Porte de Namur
☎ **02 512 24 18**
Mon.-Sat. 10.30am-6.30pm.
All the fashions from the 1950s to 1970s for both sexes with an emphasis on American cocktail dresses (€20-€50), leather coats (€90), hats (€13-€19) and genuine secondhand Levi 501s imported from the United States (around €50). You can also get a complete dinner suit for €107, crinoline dresses, purses and Hollywood-style sunglasses for those smart evening events. Should you also need something for more casual events you'll find good secondhand knitted sweaters and hippy dresses.

Idiz Bogam

76, rue Antoine Dansaert
Metro Bourse
☎ **02 512 10 32**
Mon.-Sat. noon-7pm.
It's a fairly simple step from secondhand dealing in luxury goods to designing them, and Jacqueline has made that step. In her store, near the outlets of the major designers of the Antwerp school, you'll find a

large secondhand section selling clothes for men as well as ballgowns from the 1940s to 1970s with all the accessories (€65-180), and copies of clothes and shoes from the 1970s.

Bernard Gavilan

27, rue des Pierres
Metro Bourse
☎ 02 502 01 28
www.gavilan.com
Mon.-Sat. 11am-7pm (and
Sun. 11am-7pm. Apr.-Jan.)

A technicolor atmosphere in this warehouse dedicated to the total vintage look of the 1950s to 1980s. You not only discover a Christian Lacroix coat for €100, a Levi's 501 or a blouson-style jacket at €20, new fifties court-shoes and a Sunair plastic travel bag, but also lamps, furniture and earthenware from the same period. The prices are absolutely rock-bottom, the choice very varied and the stock constantly replenished by this secondhand clothes expert.

Les Enfants d'Édouard

175-177, avenue Louise
Trams 93-94 (Defacqz)
☎ 02 640 42 45
Mon.-Sat. 10am-6.30pm.

Les Enfants d'Édouard, the crème de la crème of secondhand outlets, fills two mansions, one for women, the other for men. Inside you'll encounter only high-class punters who've dropped in for an Armani suit, a Boss coat, a Chanel suit or a Gaultier dress. Even the accessories have labels (jewelry by Christian Lacroix, Hermès ties). None of the items is more than two years old and all are, it goes without saying, in excellent condition.

Ramón & Valy

19, rue des Teinturiers
Metro Bourse
☎ 02 511 05 10
Mon.-Sat. 11am-7pm.

In Ramon and Valy's store you'll find unique designer items (Chanel, Lanvin, YSL, Dries Van Noten) secondhand for around €50, as well as new

vintage or used clothes from the 1950s to 1980s for adults and children of both sexes. Sallick jeans at around €50, check jackets and coats with fake fur collars.

Le Temps des Cerises

197, chaussée d'Ixelles
Bus 71 (Fernand Cocq)
☎ 02 646 02 19
Mon.-Sat. 11am-7pm,
except Wed.

The perfect address for women from 25 to 50 who like to renew their wardrobe frequently. Here you'll find neither brands nor vintage but good quality, relaxed clothes, in good condition and just a few seasons old. The store has an 'everything at the same price' policy, that is a T-shirt for €5, sweaters, skirts for €9, coats for €25. If you rummage around a little, you can find real bargains.

Boutique de Caroline

27, rue de l'Amazone
Bus 54 (Trinité)
☎ 02 537 30 03
Mon.-Sat. 10am-6pm.

Designer clothes in top condition for children and mothers-to-be, as well as items from the Jules et Julie and Hilde & Co collections. sporting Geluck's cat. Some good bargains, too, among the secondhand toys.

AMANDINE

If you want to be the belle of the ball, either at your wedding, or just at an evening out dancing, but you've only got a limited budget, you can hire your outfit here. There are wedding dresses fit for a princess, with crinolines, trains, tulle sewn with pearls and lace for €250; taffeta cocktail dresses and superb costume jewelry and evening purses.

150, rue Defacqz
☎ 02 539 17 93
Trams 81-82-91-92
(Janson)
Mon.-Fri. 10.30am-6pm,
Sat. 10.30am-5pm.

Designer outlets,
the art of bargain hunting

You don't have to wait for the sales to come round to treat yourself to designer goods. In these stores you can buy two or three garments for the price of one, and they won't be more than a season old. Set aside at least one suitcase to take your weekend's purchases home with you, and if you're buying discount furniture, remember it may be the transportation home that costs the most.

Le Chien du Chien & Les Puces du Chien

50A, quai des Charbonnages and 2, rue du Chien-Vert
Metro Comte de Flandres
☎ 02 414 84 00
Mon.-Sat. 10am-6pm.

This former foundry is the home of Le Chien Vert and

offers a wide range of materials and shades ranging from its own collections to Indian textiles. Le Chien du Chien tends to be classier with Jacquard cloths, damask cloths, silks (from €27 per m²). As for the Puces du Chien ('dog's fleas') you'll surely be itching to buy something here, when you discover unlabeled offcuts from rolls of designer material from €2 per m² (sq. yard).

Dod Femme

44, chaussée de Louvain
Metro Madou
☎ 02 218 24 68
Mon.–Fri. 10am-6.30pm,
Sat. 9.30am-6.30pm.

The most low-key shop of all time. There is no effort at interior design, and morose sales assistants, yet it does a

roaring trade. Of course all the brands (including big names like Chantal Thomass and Cardin) are sold at a minimum 50 percent discount. The stock is all last season's or last year's collections, in good condition, all lumped together for the browser's pleasure, particularly during the sales period when it's all even cheaper. What more could you ask for?

Dod Homme

16, chaussée de Louvain
Metro Madou
☎ 02 218 04 54
Mon. –Fri. 10am-6.30pm,
Sat. 9.30am-6.30pm.

Following the enormous success of their women's shop, Dod have taken on the men's market. Calvin Klein and Ralph Lauren at bargain prices, designer shoes, singlets and swimsuits, superb Laurentis and Hechter jackets and leather jackets (for €125!). Not forgetting discounted Samsonite luggage for carrying home all your purchases.

Dod Junior

41, chaussée de Louvain
Metro Madou
☎ 02 217 20 24
Mon.-Fri. 10am-6.30pm,
Sat. 9.30am-6.30pm.

You begin to wonder why you should go to Jacadi, Donaldson or Ale Oli to pay twice the price. The packaging here isn't so fancy and the choice is more haphazard, but you'll have all the fun of the hunt while the kids will have a whale of a time playing hide and seek in this unconventional store.

G. N. A. P.

12-14, rue du Beffroi
Bus 61 (Chasseurs-Ardennais) or Metro Diamant
☎ 02 732 84 73
Mon.-Fri. 10am-6pm,
Sat. 10am-6.30pm.

If you love Max Mara but haven't got the patience to wait for the sales, items from the catwalks and press shows are sold 40 percent cheaper all year round. The store is spotless and busy, the stock continually

renewed and you'll also find (even cheaper) unsold or bankruptcy stock, sub-brands of Max Mara and designs by Marina Rinaldi.

Underprice

35, chaussée de Bruxelles
Trams 18-52 (St Denis)
☎ 02 376 72 44
www.underprice.be
Mon.-Sat. 10am-6pm.

You have to search a little to find really good bargains, but you can buy four articles (Rue Blanche, Sandwich, Kahan, System, etc.) for €15! Although there is less choice for children and men, you can still dress the whole family at minimal expense. New deliveries every Wednesday.

Degrif

47-49, rue Simonis
Bus 54 (Trinité)
☎ 02 537 53 04
Mon.-Sat. 10.30am-7pm.

Here you'll find the major brands of Italian and French shoes at half price. Everything on sale is new, either from bankruptcy sales or ends of lines, and comes in all sizes. There are handmade styles for men, lovely leather shoes for women and sports styles for children: something for all the family. No wonder the shop is always crowded.

Dépôt Design

19, quai du Hainaut
Metro Comte de Flandre
☎ 02 502 28 82
Tue.-Sat. 10.30am-6.30pm.

This is an old printworks where contemporary furniture, designed by major Italian and Belgian designers, is sold at a discount. Furniture and items from exhibitions, ends of lines and imports direct from the factory, all new or nearly new. The place to buy a small lamp, bookshelf or sofa.

La Vaisselle au Kilo

8, rue Bodenbroek
Bus 48 (Grand-Sablon)
☎ 02 513 49 84
Mon.-Fri. 10am-6pm,
Sat.-Sun. 10am-6.30pm.

This warehouse, at the back of a yard near Sablon, sells crockery by the kilo! Plates, cups, glasses, Arques crystal, stainless-steel cutlery are bought directly from the factory, so that the prices are 20 to 30 percent cheaper than in supermarkets. Another advantage is that this shop avoids selling ends of lines so you can always re-match your set. You'll also have the pleasant surprise of finding the Président dinner set (also sold at Habitat) being sold by weight (from €5.80 a kilo).

Bookstores

The residents of Brussels have always had a fascination and need for images that transcend language barriers. For this reason, pride of place in the bookstores goes to illustration. You'll find art books, comics, photographic magazines, lithographs, postcards and reproductions of every kind, even images printed on objects.

Chapitre XII

12, avenue des Klauwaerts
Bus 71 (Macau)
☎ **02 640 51 09**
Tue.-Sat. 1.30-6pm.

It is on the ground floor of a magnificent mansion built in 1906 by her grandfather along the banks of the Ixelles ponds

that Monique Toussaint has set up a very welcoming bookstore-cum-gallery. On the tables are new literary works, bestsellers, art books and cookery books that appeal to her. On the picture rails, graphic and photographic works of great sensitivity by Belgian and European artists. The cherry on the cake is a schedule of appearances by key figures in the literary world. Get information by phone and book your seat.

Passa Porta

46, rue A. Dansaert
Metro Bourse
☎ **02 226 04 54**
www.passaporta.be
Tue.-Sat. 11.30am-7pm.
The international house of literature, opened in 2004, provides a new cultural oasis

in the very heart of the city. A showcase for Belgian and foreign literature, Passa Porta is a place to meet writers and artists from around the world, to read the international press and literature in many languages, to discover Belgian authors and to share diverse visions of the world.

Brüsel

100, boulevard Anspach
Metro Bourse
☎ **02 511 08 09**
www.brusel.com
Mon.-Sat. 10.30am-6.30pm.
Sun. noon-6.30pm.

Brüsel is synonymous with *Schuiten* which means 'quality comics'. The mezzanine houses a permanent exhibition of signed and numbered screen prints while on the ground floor there are 5,500 new and advance issue titles and some merchandise (watches, purses, lighters) with images of Corto Maltese and Bilal's heroes.

La Bande des Six Nez

**179, chaussée de Wavre
Bus 6 (Parnasse)
☎ 02 513 72 58
Mon.-Sat. 10.30am-7pm.**

Everyone gets a 20 percent discount here. As well as a wide range of comics from around the world, there's a secondhand section and a few collector's items which are shown only to people who express an interest. It's a shame that the store's expansion seems to have been used entirely for the sale of models and other comic-strip merchandise.

The largest choice of comics (30,000 titles available) in this store where a 20 percent discount is systematically applied to the cover price. Apart from the enormous stock of spin-off merchandise from comics (posters, figurines, etc.), you can also find a section devoted to children from 0 to 6 years old with books, toys and creative workshops (first Saturday morning in the month). For exhibitions of original plates by an illustrator, the house prints books with sketches and numbered silkscreen printings.

Filigranes

**38-39, avenue des Arts
Metro Arts-Loi**

Posada

**29, rue de la Madeleine
Metro Gare Centrale
☎ 02 511 08 34
Tue.-Sat. 10am-12.30
and 2-6pm.**

Here you'll find everything, or nearly everything, related to the history of art. The three floors of this narrow building are filled from floor to ceiling with rare and luxury editions, secondhand and out-of-print books and recent and old catalogues. The sales staff have encyclopedic knowledge and, if the work you want isn't on the shelves, they'll scour the world to find it for you.

La Bulle d'Or

**124-128, boulevard Anspach
Metro Bourse
☎ 02 513 01 86
www.multibd.com
Mon.-Sat. 10.30am-7pm,
Sun. 12.30-6.30pm.**

ALSO

Tropismes, a fine place for literary emotions, p. 40; **Peinture fraîche**, a small bookshop devoted to architecture and fine arts, p. 58; **The Art Home**, all the catalogs from auction rooms the world over, p. 51.

**☎ 02 511 90 15
www.filigranes.be
Mon.-Fri. 7am-7pm,
Sat. 9.30am-7pm,
Sun. 10am-6pm.**

This is both one of the best-stocked bookshops in the capital (120,000 titles), and a very friendly place with plenty of reading corners and games for adults as well as for the young. The café and winebar welcome magazine and newspaper readers. In the week, there are also concerts and meetings with authors, for those who'd like to practice their French.

Univers Particulier

**194, chaussée de Charleroi
Tram 92 (Faider)
☎ 02 538 17 77
Mon.-Sat. 10am-6.30pm.**

If you're interested in the occult, dowsing, radionics and magnetism, or you believe in tarot cards, astrology and numerology and you'd like to know what happens when we die, then pay Univers Particulier a visit. Put your thinking in a positive mode, buy some incense with special powers and dive into this strange world at the frontiers of reality.

Underwear,
from bras to boxers

Use your weekend as an excuse to take the man in your life to a lingerie store. He can't fail to respond to the delicate, sophisticated, sensuous articles on offer, whether made from silk or satin. In return you can always buy him those silk pyjamas or designer underwear he's been secretly dreaming about.

Eva Luna

41, rue du Bailli
Trams 93-94
(Lesbroussart)
☎ 02 647 46 45
Mon.-Sat. 10.30am-6.30pm.

A whole range of suggestive

lingerie to seduce your playmate. Lingerie by Chantal Thomass, sensuous Arianne nightdresses, lovely vinyl and leather corsets (Argento Vivo) or hand-painted ones (Revanche de la Femme), a very romantic embroidered collection with satin braids bearing the Eva Racheline signature, or else the Italian Cor range, younger and less costly. Little extravagances from €133 to €330 maximum (basques and corsets), these are things that should be bought for you. There are also ideas for dressing your man in smart, seamless underwear.

Stijl Underwear

47, rue Antoine Dansaert
Metro Bourse
☎ 02 514 27 31
Mon.-Sat. 10.30am-6.30pm

The place to buy original, unusual and funky lingerie for women and men in a store whose interior screams 'design.' A selection of the most exclusive styles from each brand, including a bra made of real wire by André Sarda and a pair of orange men's briefs with little pockets Nightshirts you could just as well wear during the day, silk pyjamas and well-cut swimwear, and you even get to try them on in cubicles worthy of a movie star.

Dod Lingerie

86, rue du Bailli
Trams 81-82 (Trinité)
☎ 02 538 38 48
Mon.-Sat. 10.30am-6.30pm

In the 'Dod' range, only lingerie was missing (see

.118), and here it is! These are ends of lines or batches of famous brand names sold at nearly 50 percent off! So, if you can find your size, don't hesitate to buy that nightdress, a small lace set with a famous label that won't cost you more than €30, or even a swimsuit at the start of summer.

Pierrel

6-10, galerie du Centre
Metro Bourse
☎ **02 223 10 50**
Mon.-Sat. 10.30am-6pm.

To keep up with all the latest trends from close-fitting boxers to briefs with horizontal openings, or to treat yourself to a great bathrobe, look no further. This is the only shop in Brussels to stock such a wide range of underwear, pyjamas and swimwear for men. Always in the forefront of fashion and always in good taste, it sells around twenty big names, including Calvin Klein, Armani, Hom and Olaf Benz.

Minuit Boutique

50, galerie du Centre
Metro Bourse
☎ **02 223 09 14**
Mon.-Sat. 10.30am-6.30pm.

At last, truly torrid underwear for women! Vinyl, leather and imitation leather, even some in lace, but all in the most original and outlandish styles. Are you really ready for the baby-doll nightie in black and fluorescent red plastic, the spider bra or the tulle coat that is worn over a leather corset with mega-high platform shoes? And for the uninitiated, S&M accessories; for instance rocket latex briefs (red and adjustable) from €65 to €150.

Champagne et Caviar

40, galerie du Centre
Metro Bourse
☎ **02 219 75 82**
Mon.-Sat. 11am-6.30pm.

If you're out to seduce a prince, hurry along to this little store, as it's here that the singer Fily buys her underwear. Two designers, one male, one female, have let their fantasies run riot with the aim of fulfilling yours. The result is a range of lingerie with a very hard look, leather, vinyl and imitation leopardskin or snakeskin, as well as tight-fitting miniskirts and body-hugging tops. Prices aren't excessive: you could easily kit yourself out with an ensemble from as little as €50.

Eva Luna

PATRICIA SHOP

There's nothing very flashy about the window display and yet, if you look carefully among all the lace and leopardskin prints, you're bound to find a Sloggi body stocking, an Erès swimsuit or a La Perla brassiere that will look fantastic on you. Styles from bankruptcy sales and ends of lines may be a season out of date, but when you think that you can buy three for the price of one, why deprive yourself?

158, rue Blaes
Bus 48 (Jeu-de-Balle) – ☎ **02 513 36 48**
Tue.-Sat. 9.30am-6pm, Sun. 9.30am-1pm.

Bric-a-brac,
collectibles and furniture

Hunting through the bric-a-brac stalls is the great weekend activity in Brussels. Rather than the flea market on Place du Jeu-de-Balle, which isn't very good on a Sunday, try the many junk shops and bric-a-brac sellers on Rue Blaes, Rue Haute and at the lower end of Sablon. To help you find the best antique stores, here are a few of the places we recommend.

Collectors Gallery

17, rue Lebeau
Bus 48 (Grand-Sablon)
☎ 02 511 46 13
and ☎ 0475 367 991
Fri.-Sat. 11.30am-1.30pm
and 2.30-6pm, Sun.
11.30am-1.30pm (ring bell
to enter).

This is the perfect place for collectors! Valuable perfume bottles from the 1920s to the

1950s, fantastic jewelry from 1900 to 1980, Barbie dolls, mannequins and advertising artefacts await the connoisseur. You can unearth an unusual object or a charming old dressing-table with movable mirrors.

Baden Baden

78-84, rue Haute
Bus 27 and 48 (Chapelle)

☎ 02 548 96 96
Thu.-Sat. 10am-6.30pm,
Sun. 10am-4pm.

Here you'll find early 20th-century bathroom ware and furniture in pale wood to give your modern bathroom an old-fashioned touch. This is just the place to find a traditional cast-iron bath tub with lion's paws for feet (€1,810) or a beautiful porcelain sink (€20).

À la page

2, rue du Prévôt
Bus 54 or tram 81 (Trinité)
☎ 02 537 33 04
Mon.-Sat. 11am-6.30pm.
The furniture is like the pretty tiles in this shop, somewhat

faded and antiquated. Complete *trousseaux* with linen tablecloths, embroidered sheets and batiste handkerchiefs, bath towels, country furniture, horn cutlery, old Thermos flasks and big leather suitcases to carry away all your treasures.

Au Beurfin

249, rue Haute
Bus 20-48 (Jeu-de-Balle)
☎ 0475 6024 88
Every day except Sat.
10.30am-4.30pm.

This former grocery store is the ideal place to seek out a beautiful piece of furniture, a wooden ladder, a coat rack, and many more charming, practical and inexpensive items. And if hunting around for antiques gives you an appetite, you can sit down at one of the five tables to enjoy good home-style cooking based on vegetables, bread and meat (Mon.-Fri. 12-2.30pm).

Les Caves des Minimes

59, rue des Minimes
Bus 48 (Grand-Sablon)
☎ 02 344 99 36
Tue. and Thu.-Sat. 11am-6pm, Sun. 11am-3pm.

These attractive 18th-century cellars are laid out like an old residence. On plain and graceful antique furniture, objets d'art and knickknacks are displayed, while paintings, drawings and well-framed prints are hung on the walls. There is no pomp or

pretension here, and you'll be pleasantly surprised at the price-tickets attached to each item, which couldn't be more reasonable.

Curiosités

24, rue de Rollebeek
Bus 48 (Grand-Sablon)
☎ 02 343 48 11
and ☎ 0475 813 646
www.curiosities.be
Every day except Mon.
10am-noon and 2-4pm or
by appointment.

An Aladdin's cave of curios from the days of the humanists. Old scientific instruments can be found next to the

reproduction of a human eye enlarged a hundred times, anatomical section of a cicada and an adder preserved in formaldehyde. It's difficult to tear yourself away from the rare objects piled up in heaps.

Papiers d'Antan

19, rue de l'Hôpital
Bus 48 (Saint-Jean)
☎ 02 511 24 70
Tue.-Fri. 1.30-6pm,
Sat. 10am-6pm.

Posters, prints, old share certificates, menus, sheet music, magazines, postcards, religious pictures and old iron chests. Items to entrance any paper lovers who aren't looking for in the latest news – the most recent document here dates from 1950!

Passage 125 Blaes

125, rue Blaes
Bus 20/48 (Chapelle)
☎ 02 503 10 27
Mon.-Sat. 10am-6pm
(Mon. and Fri. until 5pm),
Sun. 10am-5.30pm.

There are about 30 antique dealers gathered in this passageway on several floors. Every century and specialty can be found here from the 18th century to 1970s design. If you are looking for a lamp, a wardrobe, old tiles or salvaged bathroom appliances, it is among this heap of things that you should nose around and have a good look!

BARGAIN HUNTING ON A SUNDAY

Apart from Place Jeu-de-Balle and Sablon, here are some places for secondhand goods aficionados: Place Saint-Lambert in Woluwé: Bus 80 (Voot), every first Sunday in the month (6am-1pm), the smartest flea market in the capital; Rue Ropsy-Chaudron in Anderlecht: Bus 87/ tram 62 (Abattoirs) (7am-1pm) under the covered cattle market; Place Saint-Denis in Forest: Tram 18 (Saint-Denis) (8am-1pm), the harvest from attic clearances.

Objects
from around the world

If, on your travels, you've dreamed of bringing home a traditional Korean cabinet, the gates of a fallen rajah's palace, an enormous Chinese jar or a *zellije* tray, all these objects are gathered here. Displayed in magnificent settings the prices are reasonable if you take into account the craftsmanship and transportation.

Rambagh

64-70 and 100 rue Haute
Bus 48 (Chapelle)
☎ **02 502 25 20**
Mon.-Sat. 10am-6.30pm,
Sun. 10am-6pm.
If you feel like a change of scenery then you'll like Rambagh. Here the items of furniture and artifacts are inspired by the palaces of the

maharajahs in Jaipur. They are a blend of British refinement and Indian soul, and are based on Chinese and Korean designs. Teak, mahogany, buffalo leather, mother-of-pearl, all call to mind the luxury and simplicity of colonial art. Everything is at very moderate prices.

Chine antique

8, rue Ernest Allard
Bus 48 (Grand-Sablon)
☎ **02 512 23 01**
Tue.-Fri. 1-6pm,
Sat. and Sun. 11am-6pm.
Traditional furniture from the depths of the Chinese countryside, restored and occasionally adapted to the

requirements of life in Europe. Their purity of line is not unlike that of contemporary design and the wedding cupboards, consoles and low tables in natural or lacquered elm are no more expensive than furniture from Ikea. At these prices, why deprive yourself?

Le Jardin de Julie

214 bis, chaussée de Wavre
☎ **02 646 46 75**
Bus 34/80 (Parnasse)
Tue.-Sat. 10am-6.15pm.

The Tuscan ceramics of Impruneta, the Rolls Royce of garden pottery, in different shapes and sizes: from large pots with garlands, to jardinières and round pots with cherubs. The items are intrinsically resistant to frost and comparatively highly priced (around €87), but they're worth it as a long-term investment. There are also lovely and less expensive ceramics from Florence and Siena decorated with glazed lemons (€57) and a wide range of 19th-century-style lamps by Maxime Pradier. The beautiful bronze fountains from €210 are also worth a look.

Alizari

13, rue du Lombard
Metro Bourse
☎ 02 511 15 23
Mon.-Sat. 10am-7pm.

In this smart ethnic shop, the choice of Indian silver jewelry is exceptional. Antique pieces to be worn or treasured or recent creations at very reasonable prices (rings from €7.50, necklaces from €45). You can also find an original line in clothes, created by Patricia Mouvet. The dresses start at €70.

La Caravane passe...

2, rue de Tamines
Bus W (Place L. Morichar)
or Metro Horta
☎ 02 538 05 90
Wed.-Sat. noon-6.30pm.

The best of Moroccan craft is gathered in this shop lit by scores of wrought iron and colored glass lanterns. You may be tempted by the Akkal earthenware crockery made in Marrakech, the small stools and the tables in *zellige* mosaics (from €100), the tea glasses (€3), the jars, mirrors

and woolen carpets in sparkling colors, not forgetting the vast choice of photograph frames and lamps. The table tops are made to measure.

Nuhr Nebi

101, rue Blaes
55, rue Haute
Bus 48 (Chapelle)
☎ 02 514 07 17
Every day except Wed. 10.30am-6pm.

A wide range of lamps and shelf units in wrought iron alongside kilims, Indonesian cupboards with drawers, Afghan chests (€480) and Tuareg jewelry. There are real

finds here, like the magnificent baroque glass balls (€5-11) and Tibetan balls made of horn and ebony.

Citizen Dream

42, rue du Marché aux Herbes
Metro Gare Centrale
☎ 02 502 67 17
Every day 10.30am-6.30pm.
In this fair-trade store, the products are manufactured in India by craftsmen whose skill is fairly rewarded. A mix of the traditional and the more modern, the lacquered bowls, boxes made of horn and wood, costume and silver jewelry (from €5), silk and cashmere scarves (from €15 to €100) will tempt you with their colors, shapes and affordable prices.

Old and New Trading

7A, quai au Bois-de-Construction
Metro Sainte-Catherine
☎ 02 219 42 92
Sat.-Sun. 10.30am-6.30pm.
This huge store has a jumble of furniture and objects from Indonesia, Rajasthan, Morocco and Iran. Just the place to find Planteur armchairs at good prices, a wardrobe in the Dutch colonial style or a teak divan. Equally beautiful are the ikaté fabrics, the wrought-iron wall lights, the ground glass crockery and a thousand and one other wonders.

TEAK: LOOK FOR THE GREEN LABEL

In recent years this hardwood, which is impervious to rot, has acquired a popularity that may well cause its demise. The indiscriminate felling of the forests of Asia, which are not yet protected by law, threatens the survival of the species. So, before you buy a piece of teak furniture, check where the wood comes from. If it isn't old wood that's been reused it must show the green label that guarantees it's from a properly managed plantation.

Practicalities

Where to go

You'll find the highest concentration of cafés, restaurants and trendy clubs near Grand-Place, around Place Saint-Géry and La Bourse. This is where you should go if you want to have a drink or dance, particularly if you don't have transportation. Sablon is another very lively area (full of the young and smart) in the early evening, particularly in summer. 'Matonge', the Congolese quarter near Porte de Namur, echoes to the tropical rhythms of drums late into the night. There's always

plenty of atmosphere in the bars, where the immaculately-dressed locals go to have a few *mukumbusu* (beers) in the company of their *londo* (fiancées). Meanwhile the big concert halls can easily be reached either on foot or by metro, but if you want to see some avant-garde theater or cabaret in one of the various small venues scattered all over the city, you'll need to go by cab, as public transport comes to a halt at midnight. Only the 71N bus runs Friday every 30 minutes from 12.30-3am. Information at www.stib.irisnet.be

Booking a show

To reserve a seat for the theater or ballet from overseas, use the online ticket offices on the internet or call the box office at the venue directly and they'll send you your tickets

(a credit card is indispensable). All the branches of the bookshop, FNAC, also have ticket offices where you can buy tickets for shows and exhibitions.
You can reserve by telephone using a credit card and collect your tickets from the nearest FNAC bookshop.

FNAC Bruxelles :
City 2, rue Neuve
☎ 02 209 22 39
Mon.-Sat. 10am-7pm,
(Fri. 8pm).

FNAC location
☎ 0 900 00 600
Mon.-Sat. 10am-7pm
(Sat. 4pm)
☎ 02 275 11 11
www.fnac.be
On the spot, tickets can be bought by the hotel porter. At the last minute, you can book half-price seats for a show on the same evening. Look at the offers on www.arsene50.be (see p. 9) or go directly to the Flagey ticket office (Place

FINDING YOUR WAY

Next to each address in the Where to stay, Shopping and Going Out sections, we have given details of the nearest Brussels metro, tram or bus stop.

CAFÉS

Many cafés and even restaurants open until 3am, offering their clients live music especially on Friday and Saturday nights. You can also eat some basic dishes until midnight or 1am.

The young can be seen in old fogies' cafés and you'll see drinkers in their fifties in the trendiest places and straight couples in gay bars. All have one thing in common: they drink a lot of strong beer and enjoy being out in a crowd.

Sainte-Croix) or to Théâtre du Vaudeville (13-15, galerie de la Reine), open Tue.-Sat. 12.30-5.30pm.

deserted before 12.30 or 1am. If you haven't got a membership card and you aren't going with a member, make sure you're familiar with the dress code, which may be fancy, techno or high fashion, but is always original. Prices vary from night to night and club to club, though they're always higher on Saturday night (€5-€15).

Clubbing

To put your finger on the pulse and find out where to go to party all night, listen to radio Pure FM (101.1 FM) Friday at 2.30pm (www.purefm.be) or look at the comprehensive diary of events on www.noctis.com, www.boups.com and www.next-party.be. In summer, www.gazon.be will tell you about the free open-air events on Fridays and Saturdays in the Brussels parks (10pm to 5am). The trendy bars, an indispensable port of call before the scene hits the clubs on a Saturday night, are also busy in the week with drinkers who go for the sounds and to check out the local DJs. The clubs open their doors at 11pm, but they're totally

What to wear

If you're intending to spend an evening out at the opera, eating in a star-rated restaurant or even listening to a concert at the Palais des Beaux-Arts, don't forget to include your evening dress or smart suit and tie in your baggage.

Personal safety

Brussels isn't generally a dangerous place, by day or by night. Of course, like other big cities, it has its share of pickpockets, who operate in the subway and other crowded places, but if you use a little common sense, you shouldn't have any trouble. All the same, if you're on foot, it's a good idea to avoid passing through Place Anneessens late at night, and the same goes for the areas around the Gare du Nord and the Gare du Midi stations.

Night-shops

For night owls, there are the White-night stores and all-night Asian grocery stores. Naturally you'll find them a little more expensive than the supermarkets by day.

CULTURAL CALENDAR

Try and get hold of the monthly magazine **Kiosque**, (www.kiosque.be) which is on sale in Belgian bookstores. This gives you the best information on forthcoming events of every kind, the most fashionable bars and restaurants and the hippest clubs, along with some amusing short articles. The newspapers **Le Soir** and **La Libre** have a Wednesday supplement, which carries the full programme of the week's cultural events. Complete listings of the week's events can be found in the English-language weekly magazine, **The Bulletin**, which comes out on Wednesdays. You can also find **Zone 02** and **Agenda**, two free papers with information and addresses for going out. Finally, there are the websites to consult: www.agenda.be; www.netevents.be; www.idearts.be; www.quefaire.be; www.ebru.be

Theater, dance, music and night cafés

1 - Théâtre National
2 - Bruxelles la nuit
3 - Botanique

From €8.50. See p. 49 for the Bozar pass.

This building, which was designed by Victor Horta, is home to the Brussels Philharmonic Society, which stages concerts of orchestral music all year round as well as recitals, chamber music and early and contemporary music during the Ars Musica festival. Most of the concerts are performed by the Belgian National Orchestra, but internationally renowned artists and young musicians of proven talent also perform here. In May every three years out of four (violin, piano and singing) the building is the venue for the prestigious Queen Elisabeth Competition. Exhibitions and dance and theater performances can also be seen here.

Opera, concerts, theater, dance

Théâtre royal de la Monnaie

**Place de la Monnaie
Metro De Brouckère
Info: ☎ 02 229 12 11
www.lamonnaie.be
Reservations Tue.-Sat.
11am-6pm and 1 hour
before the performance
☎ 07 023 39 39
From €8 to €95.**

The reputation of Belgium's finest opera house has spread overseas, to the point where it's easier for a foreigner to book a seat from a booking center than it is for a Brussels inhabitant who isn't on the mailing list. As well as opera, it also hosts concerts and ballet performances.

BOZAR

**23, rue Ravenstein
Metro Gare Centrale
Info: ☎ 02 507 84 44
Tickets: ☎ 02 507 82 00
(Mon.-Sat. 11am-7pm)
www.bozar.be
Concerts at 8pm and Sun.
at 11am and 3pm**

Cathédrale Saint-Michel

Parvis Sainte-Gudule
Metro Gare Centrale
☎ 02 217 83 45
Entrance free.

Every Sunday at 10am there's a mass with plainsong sung in the Gothic cathedral by the Gregorian Scola and conducted by Michel Huybrechts.

Église Saints-Jean-et-Étienne-aux-Minimes

62, rue des Minimes
Bus 48 (Sablon)
☎ 02 511 93 84
Mon.-Fri. 10am-1pm.

Besides a plainsong mass every Sunday at 11.30am, this collegiate church, with its superb organs, hosts free concerts of Bach (every third Sunday of the month at 10.30am) and also performances of Mendelssohn or Handel in July and August (every day except Sunday at 12.15am). Other classical music concerts, particularly during Sablon's baroque spring festival in April, are performed on weekday evenings at 8pm.

Hôtel Astoria

103, rue Royale
Bus 29-63 (Congrès)
☎ 0900 288 77
www.astoria-concerts.be
Seats: €10

The Venetian chandeliers and gilded mirrors of the Waldorf room in one of the city's grand hotels from the Belle Époque provide the setting for concerts of chamber music every Sunday at 11am.

Chapelle des Brigittines

Petite rue des Brigittines
Bus 48 (Chapelle)
☎ 02 506 43 00
Reservations Mon.-Fri.

10am-1pm and 2-6pm
www.brigittines.be
Seats: €8.

A fine baroque chapel near Sablon, which has been converted into a performance space for concerts, theater and ballet. Dance and theater performances held in this venue during the Kunstfestivaldesarts (Arts Festival, May) and the International Bellone-Brigittines Festival (16 Aug.-4 Sep.) are unashamedly avant-garde and always first rate.

Lunchtime concerts at Musée d'Art Ancien

3, rue de la Régence
Trams 92-93-94 (Royale)
☎ 02 512 82 47
www.concertsdemidi.be
Every Wed. at 12.40pm
Seats: €6.

A program of chamber music, from the baroque period to our own times, focusing on up-and-coming Belgian composers and the winners of the Queen Elisabeth Competition. Your ticket gives you access to the museum's permanent collections.

Kaaitheater

20, place Sainctelette
Metro Yser
☎ 02 201 58 58
www.kaaitheater.be
Performances at 8.30pm
From €12.50 to €20.

A splendid spread of concerts featuring 20th- and 21st-century composers and the choreography of Mark Tompkins and Anna Teresa De Keersmaeker, among others. The program also includes avant-garde drama in Dutch, French and English.

Halles de Schaerbeek

22A, rue Royale-Sainte-Marie
Tram 92-93 (Ste-Marie)

☎ 02 218 21 07
Ticket office Mon-Fri.
2-6pm
www.halles.be
Seats: from €11 to €25.

This glass and iron structure, one of the last vestiges of 19th-century industrial architecture, has become a very trendy multimedia cultural center hosting a hip-hop festival, world music and dance.

Flagey

Place Sainte-Croix
Trams 81- 82 and bus 71 (Flagey)
☎ 02 641 20 20
Ticket office: Mon.-Sat.
11.30am-6.30pm
www.flagey.be

A radio station in 1938, the Flagey has rediscovered its vocation as a factory of sounds and images. This multicultural center has opened a dialogue between contemporary and classical, and popular and traditional, music; and has an alluring program to movie lovers.

Théâtre National

111-115, boulevard E. Jacqmain
Metro Rogier
☎ 02 203 53 03
www.theatrenational.be
Performances at 8.15pm or 8.30pm, Wed. at 7.30pm and Sun. at 3pm.
Seats: €18.

The theater of the French-speaking community in Belgium, housed since 2004 in a completely new glass building. Gives performances of French classics, opera, dance and also cabaret.

ALSO

Théâtre Toone

Classics are performed here by puppets speaking in the Brussels dialect (see p. 40).

Théâtre 140

140, av. E. Plasky
Bus 29-63 (Plasky)
☎ 02 733 97 08
www.theatre140.be

This is the place to come to see avant-garde plays and dance performances, plus a wide range of cabaret acts and concerts. A venue you can depend on for a good evening out.

Le Public

64-70, rue Braemt
Bus 29-63 (Saint-Josse)
☎ 0800 944 44
or ☎ 02 724 24 11
Rsservations Mon.-Fri.
10am-6pm, Sat. 2-6pm
www.theatrelepublic.be
Seats: €20.

Works by contemporary Belgian or Francophone playwrights, as well as perennial classics and best-selling authors in acclaimed productions. Theater buffs congregate in the restaurant after the show.

Koek's Théâtre

292, chaussée de Jette
Metro Simonis
☎ 02 428 66 79
www.koeks.be
Closed Tue. and Sun.

This is a real theater workshop where Belgian and French comics perform. On this stage, all of them are given their chances, provided that humor is present. In Koek's, the only rule is to be on time, because the shows start at 8.45pm sharp. Otherwise, before or after the show, you can have a drink or get a bite to eat at the bar of the theater workshop.

Botanique

236, rue Royale
Metro Botanique
☎ 02 218 37 22
www.botanique.be
Concerts at 8pm
From €5 to €16.

In the prestigious setting of the old orangeries and tropical greenhouses, the French community stages concerts, movies and various festivals which are always at the cutting edge of the multicultural arts.

Cirque Royal

81, rue de l'Enseignement
Metro Madou
☎ 02 218 20 15
Reservations every day
10.30am-6pm
www.cirque-royal.org
Performances at 8pm or
8.30pm.

In 1953 the Cirque Royal, built in 1879, was converted into a venue for performances of every kind: concerts, operas, dance, variety, revues and, of course, the circus.

Ancienne Belgique

110, boulevard Anspach
Metro Bourse
☎ 02 548 24 24
www.abconcerts.be

The main venue for good pop and rock concerts. Well worth a visit one night.

Espace Senghor

366, chaussée de Wavre
Bus 59-80 (Jourdan)
☎ 02 230 29 88
Ticket office Mon.-Fri.
9am-6.30pm
Performances at 8.30pm
From €10 to €16.

This showcase for world music and non-Western culture hosts theater and dance performances and concerts.

Night cafés

À Malte

30, rue Berckmans
Trams 91-92 (Stéphanie)
☎ 02 539 10 15
Every day 12am-3pm, 6pm-1am, Sat.-Sun. 4pm-1am.

All day long people drop in here

for breakfast, brunch, tea, an aperitif or a long late-night chat by candlelight. There are little notes stuck all over the walls, deep leather armchairs in which you can read the old books lying around on the shelves, a wooden mezzanine floor suspended like a cradle, lamp stands made from teaspoons and *Red Rakham's Treasure* locked away in the aquarium bar – in other words, a wonderful place you really must visit, both for the atmosphere and the decor. Just step inside and you'll see.

Les Salons de l'Atalaïde

89, chaussée de Charleroi
Trams 91-92 (Faider)
☎ 02 537 21 54
www.lessalonsatalaide.be
Every day noon-midnight.

The city's wildest interior. A vast mansion whose rooms each have a different mood. There's the Arab-Indian room with furniture from Rajasthan, the private room hung with Cordoba leather, the second floor terrace, the flying carpet suspended from the ceiling, the paintings by a Brazilian artist, the marble staircase and the Babylonian gate. Sadly the food isn't really up to scratch, but you can just stop by for a drink.

L'Amour fou

185, chaussée d'Ixelles
Bus 71 (F. Cocq)
☎ 02 514 27 09
Every day 9am-1am,
Fri.-Sat. until 2am.

The interior has had a total makeover, creating a more intimate atmosphere; a real local bar with newspapers for the clients (aged 18-30), where you can eat at any time. A local institution.

1 - À Malte
2 - Music Village
3 - Café Novo
4 - La Samaritaine

Zébra

33-35, place Saint-Géry
Metro Bourse
☎ 02 511 09 01
Every day noon-1.30am.

A large, sunny terrace that is always full in summer, ethnic music in the evenings, salad and *focaccia* any time, and reasonable prices. A varied and cosmopolitan crowd like to hang out here.

Au Soleil

86, rue du Marché-au-Charbon
Metro Bourse or Anneessens
☎ 02 513 34 30
Mon.-Sat. 10am-1am (2am Fri.-Sat.), Sun. 11am-1am.

This is a real old-fashioned café with wood paneling that brought new life to the entire area when it reopened back in 1990. A background of jazz or dance music, tables and chairs sprawling across the pedestrianized street and a friendly young clientele.

Le Fontainas

91, rue du Marché-au-Charbon
Metro Bourse or Anneessens

☎ 05 503 31 12
Every day 10.30am-1am (2am Fri.-Sat.)

Opposite the baroque façade of Notre Dame du Bon-Secours, a small convivial local bistro. The atmosphere is fashionably bohemian, but always friendly. An ideal place to stop for a soup or *plat du jour* in the day or to go for a drink in the evening against the background of soft electronic music. And there's a marvelous terrace in summer.

Roxi

82, rue du Bailli
Trams 81-82 (Trinité)
☎ 02 646 17 92
www.roxi.be
Every day 8am-1am.

Window tables on two floors, urban terrace in summer, cooking non-stop from noon till midnight, seasonal fruit cocktails, cool music at weekends played by switched-on DJs: in short, an open-minded atmosphere that attracts Eurocrats and the well-heeled residents of the Chatelain district.

Café Novo

37, place de la Vieille-Halle-aux-Blés
Bus 48 (Saint-Jean)
☎ 02 503 09 05
www.cafenovo.be
Mon.-Sat 10am-midnight, (Fri.-Sat. to 1am).

A new café in the Saint-Jacques quarter with minimalist decor and simple wooden tables. In the day, you can eat salads or the *plat du jour*, read the newspaper, and try the flavored teas at the adjacent counter. In the evenings, there's a latino atmosphere thanks to the *piscos* and other *mojitos* (€6) and some good music mixed by a DJ on Fridays.

Bars and clubs

1 - Disque-Au-Bar
2 - Le Grain d'Orge
3 - Dali's bar
4 - Java

Mon.-Sat. 8pm-3am
Concerts at 10pm.

A small café with live music patronized by jazz lovers and once a week, fans of the tango and Latino jam sessions.

Bazaar

63, rue des Capucins
Bus 48 (Jeu-de-Balle)
☎ 02 511 26 00
www.bazaarresto.be
Tue.-Sat. 7.30pm-1am, club open Thu.-Sat. 10pm-3am.

This is a popular meeting place for Belgians and French alike. In this cosy club, the atmosphere is always friendly. You can have a candlelit dinner, listen to world music or jazz concerts, watch cabaret shows and end the night in the disco patronized by fashionable clubbers (€7.50).

Live music and jazz clubs

La Samaritaine

16, rue de la Samaritaine
Bus 48 (Sablon)
☎ 02 511 33 95
Performances at 8.30pm except Sun. and Mon.

In a beautiful vaulted cellar is the Samaritaine workshop-cum-café, a literary cabaret, known all over Brussels. Classical music concerts are also given here.

La Tentation

28, rue de Laeken
Metro Sainte-Catherine
☎ 02 223 22 75

www.latentation.org
Mon.-Fri. 10.30am-midnight, Sat.-Sun. 6pm-midnight
From €5 to €15.

In this attractive industrial space, the Centre Culturel Galicien organizes concerts of folk music Friday and Saturday evenings and a *noche salsa* every first Saturday of the month (8pm). To prepare, there are salsa courses every Sunday from 6pm, followed by a Latino evening.

Sounds Jazz Club

28, rue de la Tulipe
Metro Porte de Namur
☎ 02 512 92 50

Beurscafé

20-28 rue Auguste Orts
Metro Bourse
☎ 02 550 03 50
www.beursschouwburg.be
Wed.-Sat. from 7pm.

A multi-faceted venue for urban encounters, the Beurscafé offers ethnic music concerts and avant-garde plays, and hosts various musical events. From 10pm onwards in the café next door made of steel and bare bricks, you can meet a varied intellectual crowd and fashionable multilingual young Flemish people. Great atmosphere on two Wednesday nights in the month during jamming sessions in which anyone can take part. See the website.

The Music Village

50, rue des Pierres
Metro Bourse
☎ 02 513 13 45
www.themusicvillage.com
Wed.-Sat. 6.30pm-midnight,
Concert at 9pm
From €9.50 to €17.

Next to Grand-Place, two 17th century houses harbor the Music Village, a New York-style jazz club. Wednesdays are evenings for young talent, Thursdays for latino music, on Fridays and Saturdays well-known Belgian and international stars perform. From 7pm a jazz dinner is served with hot and cold suggestions.

Le Grain d'Orge

142, chaussée de Wavre
Metro Porte de Namur
☎ 02 511 26 47
Every day 11am-3am,
Fri.-Sat. from 6pm.

A café brun ('brown café') where generations of young people have worn the wooden seats smooth while they drink strong beer. Free blues, rock and rhythm-and-blues concerts every Friday at 9.30pm (except in summer).

PP café

28, rue Van Praet
Metro Bourse
☎ 02 503 26 65
www.ppcafe.be. Every day
11am-3am, Fri.-Sat. from
6pm.

The wild foyer of the Pathé Palace, a well-known movie theater of the 1920s and 30s, has regained its old magnificence to become the 'stamcafé' for the area's trend-setters. Mirrors, columns, flowery frescoes and gorgons smile beneath their gold leaf. If you add the fact that all this is free and that cocktails cost €5 from 8-10pm, the place starts to look very appealing!

Blue Note

32, rue Defacqz
Trams 81-82-95, Bus 54
(Defacqz)
☎ 02 539 05 02
www.bluenote.be
Every day 4pm-4am.

This is the only place in Brussels where you can listen to traditional jazz, 'swing' to be more precise. In this smart and prosperous place, the atmosphere is friendly and you'll undoubtedly spend a good evening in front of a glass.

Late-night bars

Le Café Central

14, rue Borgval
Metro Bourse
☎ 0486 72 26 24
www.lecafecentral.com
Wed.-Sun. 9pm-3am, until
4am Fri. and Sat.

A new 1970s look for the café previously known as Acrobat, but still one of the best places in downtown Brussels to have a drink or dance to the groove of funky sounds. A mixed of generally fairly young crowd. There are bouncers on the door, but you don't have to pay to get in. A different clientele can be seen on Sundays for the movie showing at 8pm and for the Wednesday concerts twice a month (9pm).

Level Bar

35, place du Châtelain
Trams 81-82 (Trinité)
☎ 0496 242 627
Mon.-Sat. 3pm-3am.

Gray walls, with chrome moldings, feature in this bar. There are nightly thematic evenings for the affluent over-30s who like to dance to the sounds of the 1980s. Don't come before 1am: you'll be the only one here.

Le Soixante

60, rue du Marché-au-Charbon; Metro Bourse
Wed.-Sun. from 9pm.

A 'before-and-after' bar for taking the temperature of the capital and succumbing to its ambience. Some surprising cocktails and memorable DJs. Worth seeing and hearing.

Disque-Au-Bar

5, place du Nouveau
Marché-aux-Grains
Metro Bourse or
Ste Catherine
☎ 02 511 25 27
Wed.-Sat. 9pm-5am.
Entrance free.

JAZZ MARATHON

In addition to the excellent programs of the jazz clubs, there's a jazz marathon (last weekend in May; information on ☎ 02 456 04 94 or www.brusselsjazzmarathon.be) every year in most of the cafés of Brussels. And in June the World Music festival, Couleur Café, rings out loud and clear (www.couleurcafe.be).

An attic ambiance with black and red decor, rather frigid to start with but warms up as the night advances. A clientele aged 20 to 30 dances to different rhythms each night. Thursday it's electro-house, Friday pop music, Saturday techno-house mixed by well-known DJs. There's no dress code, and well-shaken cocktails cost €4-5.

Archiduc

6, rue A.-Dansaert
Metro Bourse
☎ 02 512 06 52
Every day 4pm-5am.

A very smart art-deco piano-bar with a somewhat stuffy clientele who sip their whiskies to a background of jazz music, sometimes played live. The place has been a Brussels institution since 1937.

Java

31, rue Saint-Géry
Metro Bourse
☎ 02 512 37 16
Mon-Thu. 5.30pm-2.30am,
Fri.-Sat. 5.30pm-4.30/5am.

This small, lively local bar, with a decor inspired by Gaudi, is patronized by French-speakers who come in for cocktails and all kinds of beers. There's great music, some of it live, and a buzzing atmosphere.

Le Belgica

32, rue du Marché-au-Charbon; Metro Bourse
☎ 02 514 03 24
www.lebelgica.be
Thu.-Sun. 10pm-3am.

With its stripped wallpaper and minimalist furniture, this is the city's first anti-interior design bar, whose decor is the work of two movie set designers. King Leopold II has a prime position from which to contemplate his cosmopolitan subjects as they enjoy a few drinks.

Bizon

7, rue du Pont-de-la-Carpe
Metro Bourse
☎ 02 502 46 99
www.cafebizon.com
Every day 6pm-2am
(weekends until 4am).

A small saloon bar serving cheap beers watched over by the bison's head on the wall. There's live blues-style music on Thursdays.

Dali's bar

35, petite rue des Bouchers
Metro Bourse
☎ 02 511 54 67
www.dalisbar.com
10.30pm-dawn, closed Sun.

A long midnight-blue corridor leads to the surrealist fantasies of Salvador Dali: you'll find soft watches dripping down the bar and sofas shaped like full-lipped mouths along with other metamorphoses. You sit surrounded by art sipping cocktails at neo-realist prices and listening to the DJ's selection, from the hits of the 1960s to house music.

Le Coaster

28, rue des Riches-Claires
Metro Bourse
☎ 02 512 08 47
Every day 8pm-5am/8am.

A superb copper bar and acid jazz ambience for connoisseurs of whisky (60 types) and vodka

(40 brands). Chat during the happy hours from 8-11pm and dance till dawn at the weekend.

Full Moon bar

7, rue de l'Aqueduc
Trams 91-92 (Janson)
www.thefullmoon.be
Sat. from 10pm.

Underground DJs with electro-techno preferences in a new black and white bar for nighthawks who want to hang in there till sunrise. Shaman, Microwave and other purveyors of the electro-tech gospel give forth in a highly charged atmosphere.

Clubbing

You Night Club

18, rue Duquesnoy
☎ 02 639 14 00
www.leyou.be
Fri.-Sat. 10.30pm-5am,
Sun. 6pm-3am
From €5 to €10.

The renowned decorator of Crobar and the ultra-cool Buddha Bar in Paris, Miguel Cancio-Martins, has here created a psychedelic 1970s setting: garish colors, columns, a monumental stairway, soft cushions and a huge dancefloor. On the program: The Noisy Boys, an evening of unadulterated house once a month (Friday) mixed by Olivier Gosseries. The rest of the time it's dance, R&B and hip hop. There is a tea dance every Sunday from 6pm to 3am for gays and lesbians.

Why Not

7, rue des Riches-Claires
☎ 02 512 63 43
www.welcome.to/whynot
Every day 11pm-6/7am
Entrance free.

One of the oldest gay nightclubs in Brussels, it has two bars,

1

1 - Café Central
2 - Disque-Au-Bar
3 - Basaar
4 - Dali's bar

3

2

4

a young and very masculine clientele that gets its kicks from trance music, as well as house, techno and even oldies. There's something for everyone, in other words.

Milk

40, rue de Livourne
☎ 02 534 26 67
www.milkclub.be
Thu.-Fri. 10pm-6am
Entrance €5.

This is the place where the glamorous denizens of the media and fashion worlds hang out. You have to make it past the doorman, the cloakroom attendant and the porter before penetrating the holy of holies. A whiter-than-white ambience, from the armchairs to the house cocktails, brought to life by the best DJs. Thursday, it's hits and underground music of the 1970s and1990s; Friday, the latest musical trends; Saturday, various dance music depending on the clientele.

Mirano Continental

38, chaussée de Louvain
☎ 02 227 39 51

www.dirtydancing.be
Wed. and Sat. from 11pm
From €5 to €10.

House, electro and new disco for 'dirty dancing' on Saturday, 'soul party' on Wednesday and other theme nights.

Fuse

208, rue Blaes
☎ 02 511 97 89
www.fuse.be
Sat. 11pm-7am and
sometimes Fri. and Sun.
€2.50 before midnight
then €8.

This club in the heart of Marolles is where the young go for techno music mixed by the best DJs from Europe and the USA. A great many theme nights and live performances publicized by flyers. A gay night is held one Sunday a month (www.lademence.com).

Chez Johnny – Le Claridge

24-30, chée de Louvain
☎ 02 227 39 99
www.chezjohnny.be
Fri. and Sat. from 11pm.

Something of the village dance hall and reminiscent of the good old days. Nostalgic thirty-somethings and more youthful types rub shoulders after getting their hands stamped at the door.

Les Jeux d'Hiver

Bois de La Cambre, chemin du Croquet
☎ 02 649 08 64
www.jeuxdhiver.be
Thu.-Sat. 10pm-5am/6am.

All the hits are played at this club for the offspring of the well-heeled residents, who drive up in their Porsches and BMWs. Even if you aren't one of them, you really should visit at least once in your lifetime.

Metric Conversion Chart

Women's sizes

Blouses/dresses

U.K.	U.S.A.	EUROPE
8	6	36
10	8	38
12	10	40
14	12	42
16	14	44
18	16	46

Sweaters

U.K.	U.S.A.	EUROPE
8	6	44
10	8	46
12	10	48
14	12	50
16	14	52

Shoes

U.K.	U.S.A.	EUROPE
3	5	36
4	6	37
5	7	38
6	8	39
7	9	40
8	10	41

Men's sizes

Shirts

U.K.	U.S.A.	EUROPE
14	14	36
$14^{1/2}$	$14^{1/2}$	37
15	15	38
$15^{1/2}$	$15^{1/2}$	39
16	16	41
$16^{1/2}$	$16^{1/2}$	42
17	17	43
$17^{1/2}$	$17^{1/2}$	44
18	18	46

Suits

U.K.	U.S.A.	EUROPE
36	36	46
38	38	48
40	40	50
42	42	52
44	44	54
46	46	56

Shoes

U.K.	U.S.A.	EUROPE
6	8	39
7	9	40
8	10	41
9	10.5	42
10	11	43
11	12	44
12	13	45

More useful conversions

1 centimeter	0.39 inches	1 inch	2.54 centimeters
1 meter	1.09 yards	1 yard	0.91 meters
1 kilometer	0.62 miles	1 mile	1. 61 kilometers
1 liter	2.12 (US) pints	1 (US) pint	0.47 liters
1 gram	0.035 ounces	1 ounce	28.35 grams
1 kilogram	2.2 pounds	1 pound	0.45 kilograms

Published by AA Travel Publishing.

First published as Un grand week-end à Bruxelles: © Hachette Livre (Hachette Tourisme), 2005
Written by Katherine Vanderhaeghe and Alix Delalande
Maps within the book © Hachette Tourisme

Published by AA Publishing, a trading name of Automobile Association Developments Limited, whose registered office is Fanum House, Basing View, Basingstoke, Hampshire RG21 4EA. Registered number 1878835.

ISBN-10: 0-7495-4836-3
ISBN-13: 978-0-7495-4836-0

English translation © Automobile Association Developments Limited 2006
Translation work by G and W Advertising and Publishing

Cover design by Bookwork Creative Associates, Hampshire
Cover maps © Automobile Association Developments Limited and Communicarta Ltd U.K.

Colour separation by Kingsclere Design and Print
Printed and bound in China by Leo Paper Products

Cover credits

Front cover : AA World Travel Library/Alex Kouprianoff; **Back cover** : Laurent Parrault

Picture credits

Laurent Parrault: p. 2, 3, 4, 10 (t.r.), 11, 12 (t.r., b.l.), 13 (c.r.), 15 (c.c.), 18, 19 (b.r.), 20, 21, 29 (c.l.), 30 (t.r., b.r.), 31 (c.c.), 32, 36, 37, 38, 39, 40 (t.l.), 41 (b.c.), 42, 43 (c.r.), 44, 45 (b.r.), 47 (t.r., c.l.), 48, 49 (c.l., b.r.), 50 (c.r.), 51, 52 (t.l., b.r.), 53 (t., c.l.), 54, 55 (t.r.), 57, 58 (b.), 59, 60 (c.r.), 61 (c.r.), 62, 63 (b.c.), 66, 67, 68, 69, 70, 71, 72, 73, 74, 75, 76, 78, 81, 82 (t.l., t.r., c.r.), 83, 84, 85, 86 (b.), 87, 88 (t.l., t.r.), 89, 90, 91 (t.r., t.r.), 92, 94 (t.l., t.r.), 95, 96 (c.r., b.l.), 97, 98 (t.l.), 99, 100, 101, 102 (t.l., t.r.), 103, 104 (t.l., b.l.), 105, 106 (t.r., b.l.), 107 (c.l., b.r.), 108 (c.l.), 110 (t.l.), 111 (c.r.), 112 (t.l.), 113, 115 (t.r.), 116 (t.l.), 118 (b.l.), 119 (b.r.), 120 (b.l.), 122 (t.l., b.l.), 123 (c.l., b.r.), 125 (t.r., b.r.), 126 (t.r.), 127, 128, 130 (t.l., t.r., c.r.), 133, 134, 136, 137.

Éric Guillot: p. 10 (t.l., b.r.), 12 (t.l.), 13 (t.c.), 14 (t.l.), 15 (t.r.), 16, 17, 19 (t.l., c.c.), 22, 23, 24 (t.r., t.l.), 25 (t.r.), 26, 27, 28, 29 (t.r.), 31 (t.l.), 40 (c.c., b.r.), 41 (t.c., c.r.), 43 (t.l., b.c.), 45 (t.r.), 46, 47 (c.r.), 49 (t.c.), 50 (t.r.), 52 (c.c.), 53 (b.r.), 55 (c.l.), 56, 58 (c.l.), 60 (b.l.), 61 (t.c., c.r.), 63 (t.c., c.r.), 64, 65, 82 (c.l.), 88 (c.l.), 96 (t.l.), 98 (t.r.), 102 (b.l.), 104 (t.r.), 106 (t.l.), 107 (t.c.), 108 (c.c.), 109 (t.r., c.l.), 110 (t.r., c.r., b.l.), 111 (t.c.), 112 (t.r., b.c.), 114 (t.l., b.r.), 115 (c.l.), 116 (t.r., b.l.), 117, 118 (t.l., t.r.), 119 (t.c.), 120 (t.l., t.r.), 121, 123 (t.r.), 124, 125 (c.c.), 126 (t.l., b.l.), 130 (c.l.).

Hachette: p. 14 (t.r., c.c.), 24 (b.c.).
Delvaux: p. 25 (b.r.), 30 (t.l.), 31 (b.r.)
Rouge Tomate © **Jasmine Van Hevel**: p. 86 (t.l.)
Tea for Two: p. 91 (c.c.)
Olivier Strelli: p. 94 (b.l.)
Rue Blanche: p. 98 (b.c.)
Dille et Kamille: p. 109 (b.c.)
Au Fil du Temps: p. 114 (t.r.)
Hom: p. 122 (t.r.)

Illustrations

Monique Prudent

A02680